go getter 2

T0386088

Workbook

Jennifer Heath with Catherine Bright

Contents

0 Get started! p.4

1 Classmates p.8

2 Fun with food p.16

Skills Revision 1&2 p.24

3 Technology for all p.26

4 Big world p.34

Skills Revision 3&4 p.42

5 Around town p.44

6 Just the job p.52

Skills Revision 5&6 p.60

7 Going places p.62

8 Having fun p.70

Skills Revision 7&8 p.78

Exam Practice 1–4 p.80

Exam Practice 5–8 p.85

Get more on Science! p.90

Get more on Geography! p.91

Get more on Art! p.92

Get more on History! p.93

Answer key p.94

Irregular verbs p.96

Get started!

0.1

1 Complete the sentences with the words in the box.

> Amy cat Elena friends ~~Lucas~~
> red Spain Tom

1. Hi, I'm _Lucas_ . I'm from _____ .
2. Hello. I'm _____ . I've got a _____ .
3. Hi. I'm _____ . My favourite colour is _____ .
4. Hello. I'm _____ . I've got a lot of _____ .

to be

+	−
I'm from Wales.	I'm not from England.
You're Spanish.	You aren't Italian.
He/She/It's ten.	He/She/It isn't thirteen.
We/You/They're friends.	We/You/They aren't friends.
?	**Short answers**
Are you from Wales?	Yes, I am. / No, I'm not.
Is he twelve?	Yes, he is. / No, he isn't.
Are they brothers?	Yes, they are. / No, they aren't.

2 Circle the correct answer.

1. Amy (isn't) / aren't eleven. She 's / 're twelve.
2. **A:** Are / Is you from Wales?
   B: Yes, I am / are.
3. We am not / aren't sisters. We 's / 're friends.
4. **A:** Is / Are they Italian?
   B: No, they isn't / aren't.

3 **Vocabulary** Complete the table with the words in the box.

> ~~Argentinian~~ August Chinese France
> Germany Italian July September Turkey

Countries	Nationalities	Months
	Argentinian	

have got

+	−
I/You've got a sister.	I/You haven't got a sister.
He/She/It's got a cat.	He/She/It hasn't got a cat.
We/You/They've got a dog.	We/You/They haven't got a dog.
?	**Short answers**
Have you got a dog?	Yes, I have. / No, I haven't.
Has he/she /it got a book?	Yes, he/she/it has. / No, he/she/it hasn't.
Have they got a cat?	Yes, they have. / No, they haven't.

4 Complete the sentences. Write the correct form of *have got*.

1. **A:** Have you ___got___ a sister?
   B: No, I _____ .
2. He _____ a dog. Its name is Rex.
3. I _____ a new bike. My bike is old.
4. **A:** _____ she _____ a cat?
   B: No, she _____ .

Vocabulary Look at the pictures. Circle the correct answer.

1 He can *play football* /(*ride a bike*).

2 She can *play the guitar* / *sing*.

3 They can *play football* / *run*.

4 You can *skateboard* / *draw*.

5 He can *speak Spanish* / *sing*.

6 I can *cook* / *swim*.

can

➕	➖
I/You can sing.	I can't sing.
He/She/It can sing.	He/She/It can't sing.
We/You/They can sing.	We/You/They can't sing.
❓	Short answers
Can you sing?	Yes, I can. / No, I can't.
Can he sing?	Yes, he can. / No, he can't.
Can they sing?	Yes, they can. / No, they can't.

Match 1–4 to a–d.

1 ☐ Elena can play   a play football.
2 ☐ Tom can   b ride a bike?
3 ☐ Can Lucas   c can't sing.
4 ☐ Amy   d the guitar.

Answer the questions for you.

1 Can you swim? _____
2 Can you cook? _____
3 Can your best friend draw? _____
4 Can your friends sing? _____

1 **Vocabulary** What can you see in the picture? Tick (✔) for *yes*.

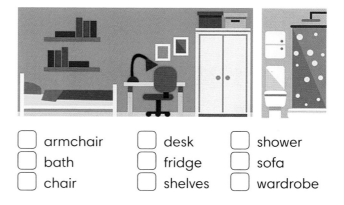

☐ armchair   ☐ desk   ☐ shower
☐ bath   ☐ fridge   ☐ sofa
☐ chair   ☐ shelves   ☐ wardrobe

there is / there are

➕	➖
There's a wardrobe.	There isn't a TV.
There are three schoolbooks.	There aren't any clothes in the wardrobe.
❓	Short answers
Is there a TV in your room?	Yes, there is. / No, there isn't.

2 **Complete the text with the words in the box.**

> Are   aren't   there   Is   ~~is~~   isn't

I've got a small bedroom. There ¹*is* a bed and
² _____ is a wardrobe in my bedroom, but
there ³ _____ a desk and there ⁴ _____
any chairs. ⁵ _____ there any shoes? Yes,
there are. They are under my bed. ⁶ _____
there a cat? Yes, there is. My cat is on my bed!

3 **Vocabulary** Look at the picture. Complete the phrases with prepositions of place.

1 a ball <u>o n</u> the wardrobe
2 a skateboard _ _ _ _ _ the wardrobe
3 clothes _ _ the wardrobe
4 a guitar _ _ _ _ _ _ the wardrobe

1 What are their names? Label the pictures.

1 _____ 2 _____ 3 _____

2 Vocabulary Look at the photo. What can you see? Tick (✔) for yes.

- ✔ dress
- ☐ coat
- ☐ hoodie
- ☐ jeans
- ☐ T-shirt
- ☐ hat
- ☐ jumper
- ☐ trousers
- ☐ jacket
- ☐ shoes
- ☐ trainers
- ☐ skirt

this, these, that, those

Singular	What's this? ➡ It's a coat.
Plural	What are these? ➡ They're trainers.
Singular	What's that? ➡ It's a hat.
Plural	What are those? ➡ They're sausages.

3 Complete the questions with *this, these, that* or *those*. Then complete the answers.

1 What's _this_ ? _____ a hat.
2 What are _____ ? _____ tennis balls.
3 What's _____ ? _____ a dog.
4 What are _____ ? _____ my trainers.

1 Vocabulary Complete the adjectives.

1 Carla is c_l_ev_er_ and pr_ _ _ _ .
2 Rocco is sm_ _l and sp_ _ty .
3 Big Al is fr_ _ _ _ly and f_n_y .

LOOK!

- put the adjectives **before** the noun
  a new hat
- adjectives are always singular
  one new hat
  two new hats.
- put *very* **before** the adjective
  The hat is *very* cool.

2 Put the words in the correct order to make sentences.

1 got I've a bike new .
   I've got a new bike.
2 helpful You're friend a .
   _____
3 hat a It's big .
   _____
4 old book is very The .
   _____
5 sister girl My is a pretty very .
   _____

Possessive adjectives

I	my	he	his	we	our
you	your	she	her	you	your
		it	its	they	their

Possessive 's

It's Big Al's home. = It's his home

3 Circle the correct word.

1 This is my mum. (Her)/ His name is Anna.
2 Tom is cool. *Her / His* hobby is football.
3 They're friends and *their / our* names are Rocco and Carla.
4 We're brothers and *your / our* hobby is sport.
5 *Dave's / Dave* best friend is John.
6 My *dad's / dads* name is Bill.

Vocabulary

1 Look at the photos. Circle the correct word.

0 (coat)/ jacket

1 armchair / sofa

2 trousers / hoodie

3 bath / shower

4 hat / T-shirt

5 fridge / wardrobe

2 Circle the odd one out.

0 big   small   (sing)   pretty
1 Argentina   November   Poland   Italy
2 Chinese   British   Turkey   Polish
3 play football   funny   swim   cook
4 February   Germany   the UK   the USA
5 skateboard   helpful   clever   old

☐/⑤

Grammar

3 Complete the short answers.

0 **A:** Have you got a brother?
   B: Yes, I *have* .
1 **A:** Has she got a dog?
   B: No, she _____ .
2 **A:** Is he old?
   B: No, he _____ .
3 **A:** Are you best friends?
   B: Yes, we _____ .
4 **A:** Can you cook?
   B: Yes, I _____ .
5 **A:** Can they draw?
   B: No, they _____ .

☐/⑤

4 Circle the correct word.

0 Hi. (My)/ Its name is Mark.
1 Look at Maria. *Her / His* hat is cool.
2 They can play football. It's *his / their* favourite hobby.
3 There *is / are* some shoes in the wardrobe.
4 There *isn't / aren't* a book on your desk.
5 **A:** What's *that / those*?
   B: It's my jacket.

☐/⑤

Communication

5 Complete the dialogue with the words in the box.

> England   from   is   ~~name~~   October
> Spanish

Anna: Hi. I'm Anna. What's your ⁰*name* ?
Carlos: I'm Carlos. Where are you from?
Anna: I'm ¹_____ the UK. What about you?
Carlos: I'm ²_____ , but I'm at school in ³_____ .
Anna: When ⁴_____ your birthday, Carlos?
Carlos: It's in ⁵_____ .

☐/⑤

Vocabulary ☐/⑩
Grammar ☐/⑩
Communication ☐/⑤
Your total score ___ / 25

Classmates

1 Look at the picture. Write the school items.

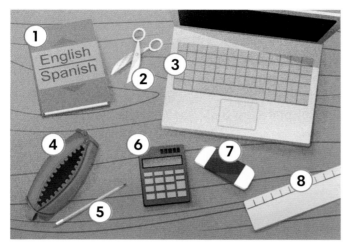

1 *dictionary*
2 _____
3 _____
4 _____
5 _____
6 _____
7 _____
8 _____

2 Find and circle eight school subjects. Then complete the sentences.

A	F	R	E	C	H	H	I	E
A	R	T	N	F	M	A	T	N
G	E	O	G	R	A	P	H	Y
O	N	M	L	A	T	H	I	L
G	C	G	I	N	H	I	S	I
R	H	E	S	S	T	T	S	S
A	I	O	H	H	I	S	O	H
P	M	U	S	I	C	Y	R	M
S	C	I	E	N	C	E	Y	A

1 I paint pictures of flowers in *Art* .
2 We learn to say *Bonjour* in _____ .
3 I learn about different countries in _____ .
4 In _____ we can use a calculator for problems.
5 We do cool experiments in _____ .
6 In _____ we sing lots of songs.
7 This book about the past is for _____ .
8 Today's grammar lesson for _____ is *I can.*

3 Complete the words.

1 I've got a new d <u>i c t i o n a r</u> y for English.
2 Where are my t_ _ _ _ _ _s? We have P.E. nex⟨
3 There are ten laptops in the C_ _ _ _ _ _r
   S_ _ _ _ _s classroom.
4 **A:** Is there any green p_ _ _t ?
   B: Yes, there's some in the art box.
5 My favourite subject is H_ _ _ _ _y because
   we learn about the past.
6 I play the piano in my M_ _ _c lesson.
7 Your m_ _ is good. Is it your Geography
   homework?
8 **A:** Where's my p_ _ _ _l c_ _e ?
   B: Is it in your bag?

4 Read about Karen and complete the informatio⟨

My name is Karen. I'm 11 years
old. My favourite subjects are P.E
and Computer Studies. I have P.E
on Monday and Wednesday and
Computer Studies on Friday.

Name: _____ *Karen* _____
Age: _____
Favourite subjects: _____
_____

5 Complete the information about you. Then write.

I rememb⟨
that!

Name: _____
Age: _____
Favourite subjects: _____
_____

My name is
_____
_____

Present Simple affirmative

+	I/You/We/They	listen to music.
	He/She/It	listens to music.

Complete the sentences with the verbs in the box.

go   goes   like   ~~likes~~   play   plays

1 My sister ___likes___ going to the cinema.
2 Frank _____ to school with his sister.
3 My parents _____ reading.
4 We _____ basketball at school.
5 I _____ to bed at 8 o'clock.
6 She _____ computer games on Sunday.

LOOK!

love → loves   eat → eats   play → plays

do → does   go → goes   watch → watches
wash → washes   study → studies   fly → flies

Rewrite the sentences about Amy and Tom.

1 I have breakfast at home.

2 I meet my friends before class.

3 I like my teachers.

1 _Amy has breakfast at home._
2 _____
3 _____

4 I love football.

5 I bring my football to school.

6 I play football with my friends.

4 _____
5 _____
6 _____

3 Complete the sentences with the correct form of the verbs.

1 The boys ___do___ (do) their homework before dinner.
2 My dad _____ (listen) to music in the car.
3 Tim and Mark _____ (play) football at the weekend.
4 Mary and her sister _____ (go) to the same school.
5 We all _____ (have) lunch in the canteen.
6 I _____ (watch) a lot of films.
7 She _____ (study) a lot for tests.
8 Marie _____ (help) me with my homework.

Adverbs of frequency

■■■■ always	**Adverb + verb**
■■■□ usually	I **never** listen to music.
■■□□ often	We **sometimes** watch TV.
■□□□ sometimes	**Adverb + to be**
□□□□ never	He is **often** late for school.
	I am **always** happy.

✹ 4 Rewrite the sentences. Use the word in brackets.

1 My mum makes a cake. (often)
   My mum often makes a cake.
2 Dad works at home. (never)
   _____
   _____
3 I am late to school. (often)
   _____
   _____

4 She does her homework in the evening. (usually)
   _____
5 They play football in the park. (always)
   _____
6 My friends are noisy in class. (sometimes)
   _____
7 My friend's jokes are good. (usually)
   _____

Extra Online Practice

Unit 1, Video and Grammar
www.myenglishlab.com

Present Simple negative

→	I/You/We/They	don't paint.
	He/She/It	doesn't paint.

don't = do not   doesn't = does not

1 Write negative sentences.

1 My sister has a hobby.
My sister _doesn't have_ a hobby.

2 They like my pictures.
They _____ my pictures.

3 David does karate.
David _____ karate.

4 My parents play tennis.
My parents _____ tennis.

5 She studies French at school.
She _____ French at school.

6 My grandad plays chess.
My grandad _____ chess.

Present Simple questions and short answers

?	Short answers
Do I/you/we/they paint?	Yes, I/you/we/they do. / No, I/you/we/they don't.
Does he/she/it paint?	Yes, he/she/it does. / No, he/she/it doesn't.

Where do you paint?
When do they paint?
How often does she paint?

2 Circle the correct word. Then answer for you. Use short answers.

1 (Do)/ Does you have a hobby?
Yes, I do. / No, I don't.

2 Do / Does your friend play sport? _____

3 Do / Does your dad paint? _____

4 Do / Does you like karate? _____

5 Do / Does your friends play chess? _____

6 Do / Does you study English on Sundays?
_____

3 Look at the table. Complete the questions with *Do* or *Does*. Then write short answers.

play football	✗	✗
like music	✔	✔
paint pictures	✔	✗
play chess	✗	✔

1 _Does_ Carla paint pictures? _Yes, she does._

2 _____ Rocco paint pictures? _____

3 _____ Rocco and Carla like music? _____

4 _____ Rocco and Carla play football? _____

5 _____ Rocco play chess? _____

6 _____ Carla play chess? _____

4 **Vocabulary** Look at the photos. Circle the correct answers.

1 (do)/ play
pottery / chess

2 do / play
the piano / the drums

3 do / play
judo / ballet

✱ 5 Complete the dialogue with the correct forms.

Bob: Hi. ¹_Do you have_ (you/have) a hobby?

Jim: Yes, I ² _____ . I paint pictures.
³ _____ (you/like) my picture? It shows my sister.

Bob: Yes, I ⁴ _____ . It's lovely.
⁵ _____ (your sister/paint) too?

Jim: No, she ⁶ _____ . She ⁷ _____ (not like) painting.

Bob: What ⁸ _____ (she/do)?

Jim: She plays the drums!

2 Asking for personal information

What's your name?
How do you spell that?
Where do you live?
What's your email address?
What's your phone number?

1 Complete the dialogue with the words in the box.

| address | day | ~~join~~ | spell | start |
| surname |

Karen: Good morning.

Mr Tims: Good morning.

Karen: I'd like to ¹ _join_ the chess club, please.

Mr Tims: OK, Karen. What's your ² _____ ?

Karen: It's Browne.

Mr Tims: How do you ³ _____ that?

Kate: It's with an E. B-R-O-W-N-E.

Mr Tims: What's your email ⁴ _____ ?

Karen: It's kbrowne@mymail.com.

Mr Tims: Thanks.

Karen: What ⁵ _____ does the club meet?

Mr Tims: It meets on Monday.

Karen: What time does the club ⁶ _____ ?

Mr Tims: At 4 p.m.

Karen: Where does it meet?

Mr Tims: It meets in Room 107.

2 Read the dialogue in Exercise 1 again. Complete the information.

After school club

Name of Club: ¹ _Chess_ Club
Day: ² _____
Time: ³ _____ p.m.
Where: Room ⁴ _____
Student: ⁵ _____ Browne
Student's email: ⁶ _____

LOOK! Email addresses
@ = "at"   .com = "dot com"
Telephone numbers
0 = "oh" or "zero"
33 = "double three"

3 Complete the questions with one word in each gap.

1 _What_'s your name?
2 _____ do you spell that?
3 _____ do you live?
4 _____'s your email address?
5 _____'s your phone number?

4 Match answers a–e to the questions in Exercise 3.

a [3] 25 Star Street, Kingston.
b [ ] Tom Flynn.
c [ ] It's 08976 335214.
d [ ] It's tom.flynn@mymail.com.
e [ ] T-O-M   F-L-Y-N-N.

5 Answer the questions in Exercise 3 for you.

1 _____
2 _____
3 _____
4 _____
5 _____

Extra Online Practice

Unit 1, Video and Communication
www.myenglishlab.com

My school

How many students have P.E. every day for two hours? Not many? Well, I always have P.E. from 2.30 to 4.30. I'm Steve and I want to tell you about my school.

My day starts early. I usually get to school at 8.00 but I'm sometimes late. Lessons start at 8.30. My favourite subject is Geography because I like maps. I don't like Art because I don't paint good pictures.

We have lunch at 12.00 and I often have chicken and chips. I never have fish and chips.

In the afternoon we have P.E. I love P.E.! We usually play football or do karate. On Friday we play basketball. My favourite sport is football because I want to play for a big team.

We finish school at 4.30. That's late for most schools. But I don't mind because I play sport every day! My sport school is great!

1 Read the text. What type of school is it about? Tick (✔).

A □
Sports School

B □
Art School

C □
Drama School

2 Read the text again. Circle the correct answer.

1 What time does Steve usually get to school?

a 　b

2 What is his favourite subject?

a 　b

3 What does Steve have for lunch?

a 　b

4 Which sport do they do on Friday?

a 　b

5 Does Steve like his school?

a 　b

3 Read the text again. Answer the questions.

1 Does Steve sometimes get to school late?
   Yes, he does.
2 Why does he like Geography? _____
3 Does he paint good pictures? _____
4 What sports does he usually do? _____
5 What does he do on Friday? _____
6 Does he finish school before 4.00? _____

4 **Vocabulary** Match words 1–8 to definitions a

1 [c] canteen　5 [ ] hall
2 [ ] classroom　6 [ ] library
3 [ ] computer room　7 [ ] playground
4 [ ] gym　8 [ ] staff room

a This is a special classroom with laptops.
b Teachers relax and mark homework there.
c You have lunch there.
d There are lots of books for extra study there.
e This is a very large room for P.E.
f This is a very large room for assembly.
g You play outside in break time there.
h You have lessons at your desks there.

1 🔊 3 Listen to Mark. Write the days of the week.

> Monday ~~Tuesday~~ Wednesday
> Thursday Friday Saturday Sunday

French: ¹_Tuesday_
Science: ²_____ and ³_____
History: ⁴_____ and ⁵_____
football: ⁶_____
chess: ⁷_____

2 🔊 3 Listen again. Circle T (true) or F (false).

1 Mark's favourite subject is French.   (T)/ F
2 Mark likes Science.   T / F
3 He likes History.   T / F
4 He plays football at school.   T / F
5 He always plays chess on Sunday.   T / F

Time expressions with *at, in, on*

AT   at 9 o'clock, at the weekend, at lunchtime

IN   in the morning

ON   on Monday, on Friday morning, on a weekday

3 Read Blanca's blog post. Circle the correct answer.

4 Look at Ken's notes. Write a blog post about his favourite day.

> name: Ken
> favourite day: Friday
> get up: 7.00
> meet friends: 7.30
> walk to school, always talk about TV
> morning: Computer Studies afternoon: P.E. (favourite subjects!)
> dinnertime: fish and chips (love!)
> evening: play basketball 8 p.m.

My name is Ken and my favourite day is _____
_____
_____
_____
_____
_____
_____
_____
_____
_____
_____

My favourite day

My favourite weekday is Tuesday.

I get up ¹(at)/ on 7.30. I meet my friends ²at / in 8 o'clock and we get the bus to school. We often talk about our favourite singers.

³On / In Tuesday, we have Music, Computer Studies and English. They are my favourite subjects! ⁴At / In the morning, we have Music. We sometimes sing and I usually play the piano.

I have pizza ⁵at / on lunchtime. Tuesday is pizza day in the canteen!

⁶In / At the evening, after school, I always do ballet.

Vocabulary

1 Match 0–5 to a–f.

0 [a] Do you read
1 [ ] In Maths we can use
2 [ ] We write games on laptops
3 [ ] Do you need a dictionary
4 [ ] I like Geography because
5 [ ] His trainers are in his bag

a Harry Potter books in English?
b because he has P.E. today.
c I think maps are very interesting.
d a calculator for problems.
e in our Computer Studies lesson.
f for your French homework?

⬜/⑤

2 Choose the correct answer.

0  Does your friend (*play*)/ *do* the drums?

1 Do you *play* / *do* chess?

2 We've got P.E. in the *gym* / *classroom* next.

3  Let's meet for lunch in the *canteen* / *library*.

4 I don't *play* / *do* karate.

5 It's time for assembly in the *staff room* / *hall*.

⬜/⑤

Grammar

3 Complete the sentences with the correct form of the verbs.

0 You _listen_ (listen) to music on the bus.
1 I _____ (play) football at break time.
2 She _____ (watch) TV before dinner.
3 John _____ (not have) a new pencil.
4 They _____ (not go) to school on Sunday.
5 We _____ (not do) pottery at school.

⬜/⑤

4 Put the words in the correct order to make sentences.

0 are We never in class noisy .
We are never noisy in class.

1 do I always ballet Monday on .
_____

2 walks to sometimes He school .
_____

3 I play never football school before .
_____

4 have Do sandwich a you lunch for ?
_____

5 she late How often is in morning the ?
_____

⬜/⬜

Communication

5 Write questions to these answers.

0 A: _How old are you?_
  B: 12.
1 A: _____
  B: I'm Paul Harris.
2 A: _____
  B: H–A–R–R–I–S.
3 A: _____
  B: 22 North Street, Oldtown.
4 A: _____
  B: It's 02461 431948.
5 A: _____
  B: It's pharris@mymail.com.

⬜/⬜

Vocabulary ⬜/⑩
Grammar ⬜/⑩
Communication ⬜/⑤
Your total score ▓ / 25

Extra Online Practice

Unit 1, Language Revision
www.myenglishlab.com

Word blog: My things

1 About me Write the school subjects.

	Monday	Tuesday	Wednesday
9 am	1 _____	2 _____	1789 3 _____
10 am	4 _____	5 _____	6 _____
11 am	Bonjour! 7 _____	8 _____	Hello! 9 _____

2 My chat room Complete the comments.

We've got French and Maths together. Can I use your ¹d_____y and your ²c_____r?

Danny

Art on Monday! Great way to start the week. We need blue and red ³p_____ts this Monday, so don't forget! And wear ⁴t_____rs for P.E.!

Trisha

Computer Studies this year at last! And we have new ⁵l_____ps in the computer room!

Bob

The bookshop has new ⁶p_____l c_____es! And they are really cheap! Pens, ⁷p_____ls, a ruler, ⁸s_____rs and two rubbers inside!

Maria

3 Get more Circle the correct answer.

Cool things in my school.

1 This is our old school *bell / instrument*.

2  This *bell / instrument* is the school piano.

3 This is my *science program / experiment*.

4 Check out my computer *program / experiment*.

Get more words

Be quiet, please!

Who's speaking? Match sentences 1–6 to people A–F.

1 I usually play the drums!
2 I do ballet on Mondays.
3 I play basketball at 4 p.m.
4 We often play chess.
5 I do karate on Mondays.
6 I sometimes do pottery.

Fun Spot

2 Fun with food

2.1 Vocabulary

1 Match the photos to the food products.

Good Food

	1	2	3
A			
B			
C			

1 bread _A1_   6 potatoes _____
2 cereal _____   7 salad _____
3 cheese _____   8 yoghurt _____
4 chicken _____   9 orange juice _____
5 fish _____

2 Complete the sentences with the words in the box.

> biscuit   ~~cereal~~   fruit   pasta
> sandwich   tuna

1 I usually have _cereal_ for breakfast.
  I like corn flakes best.
2 Have we got any bread? I want to make a ham _____ .
3 I like _____ . It's my favourite fish.
4 Can I have a chocolate _____ with my tea?
5 Apples are good for you. They're my favourite _____ .
6 Let's have _____ for dinner. I hope you like spaghetti.

3 Look at the picture. Complete the dialogue with one word in each gap.

Pam: That ¹_salad_ looks nice. Do you want some?
Rob: Yes, please. I love tomatoes. A ham ²_____ fo you?
Pam: No, thank you, but can I have some ³_____ ?
Rob: Of course. Do you like ⁴_____ ? There are som long ones in the hot dogs.
Pam: Not really. I prefer ⁵_____ . It's my favourite m
Rob: Any drinks? Orange ⁶_____ or ⁷_____ ?
Pam: Nothing at the moment. But I want to try those ⁸_____ with lots of jam!

4 Circle the correct answer.

I have ¹(breakfast)/ lunch at 7 a.m. I like ²fruit / vegetables so I always have an apple at school. I have ³dinner / lunch at 7 p.m. with my mum and dad. Mum often cooks chicken because it's our favourite ⁴fish / meat. Today mum is busy so my dad is making cheese ⁵bread / sandwiches for us. I sometimes have ⁶a yoghurt / pasta afterwards. I put a banana in it.

5 Complete the table with food words.

I rememb that!

Fruit and vegetables	Food from animals	Meals
apples	_cheese_	_pancakes_
_____	_____	_____
_____	_____	_____

Countable and uncountable nouns

Countable nouns	Uncountable nouns
an egg, a strawberry	sugar, milk
two lemons	—
some sausages	some sugar, milk

some / any

	Countable nouns	Uncountable nouns
+	There are some sausages.	There is some milk.
–	There aren't any sausages.	There isn't any milk.
?	Are there any sausages?	Is there any milk?

1 Vocabulary What can you see in the picture? Tick (✔).

- [✔] apple
- [ ] butter
- [ ] chocolate
- [ ] egg
- [ ] flour
- [ ] jam
- [ ] lemon
- [ ] milk
- [ ] sausage
- [ ] strawberry
- [ ] sugar

2 Complete with the words in Exercise 1.

Countable

apple
_____
_____
_____
_____

Uncountable

_____ _____
_____ _____
_____ _____

Circle the correct answer.

My pancake recipe has ¹a / an / – flour, ²a / an / – egg, ³a / an / – milk and ⁴a / an / – butter. For the topping I like ⁵a / an / – banana and ⁶a / an / – cream.

4 Complete the sentences with some or any.

1 There aren't ___any___ apples left.
2 There are _____ biscuits in the cupboard.
3 There isn't _____ yoghurt, but there is _____ ice cream.
4 There are _____ strawberries in the fridge, but there isn't _____ sugar.

5 Complete the questions and short answers.

1 __Is__ there __any__ sugar? ✔ __Yes, there is.__
2 ____ there ____ apples? ✔ _____
3 _____ butter? ✘ _____
4 _____ bananas? ✘ _____
5 _____ tuna? ✔ _____

✱6 Look at the shopping list. Complete the dialogue with the words in the box.

an	~~any~~	are	aren't	is	some	there

1 litre milk   butter   chocolate
6 eggs   flour   4 bananas

Tom: What's on the shopping list? Does mum want ¹ ___any___ chocolate?

Matt: Yes! There are ² _____ bananas too.

Tom: And ³ _____ there any eggs on the list?

Matt: Yes, ⁴ _____ are.

Tom: What about ⁵ _____ orange?

Matt: No. There ⁶ _____ any oranges. Look! There ⁷ _____ some butter on the list. It's a list for pancakes!

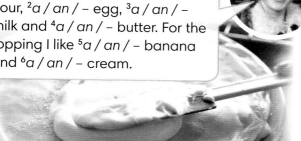

Extra Online Practice

Unit 2, Video and Grammar
www.myenglishlab.com

How much …? How many …? a lot of

Countable nouns	Uncountable nouns
How **many** apples are there?	How **much** water is there?
There are **a lot of** apples.	There is **a lot of** water.
There are **six** apples.	There are **four** bottles of water.

1 Complete the questions and answers.

1 How _many_ bananas _are_ there?
   There are five bananas.

2 How _____ chicken ____ there?
   _____ a lot of chicken.

3 How _____ sausages ____ there?
   _____ six sausages.

4 How _____ rice ____ there?
   _____ a lot of rice.

5 How _____ sandwiches ____ there?
   _____ two sandwiches.

2 Complete the dialogue with the words in the box.

> a   are   lot   many   much   ~~much~~

Big Al: I'm hungry. How ¹ _much_ food is there?
Rocco: There's a ² _____ of food! Don't worry!
Big Al: How ³ _____ biscuits are there?
Rocco: There are ⁴ _____ lot of biscuits.
Big Al: And how ⁵ _____ chocolate is there?
Rocco: There ⁶ _____ six bars of chocolate.

3 **Vocabulary** Complete the words.

1 b**a**r   3 c_n   5 j_r
2 b_ttl_   4 c_rt_n   6 p_ck_t

4 Complete the expressions with the words in Exercise 3.

1 a ___bar___ of chocolate

2 a _____ of jam

3 a _____ of juice

4 a _____ of water

5 a _____ of biscuits

6 a _____ of cola

5 Complete the dialogue with one word in each gap.

Lara: ¹ _How_ much chocolate is there?
Nick: There ² _____ two ³ _____ o(f) chocolate.
Lara: How ⁴ _____ juice is there?
Nick: ⁵ _____ are two ⁶ _____ of ju(ice)
Lara: OK. How ⁷ _____ apples are the(re)
Nick: Just one. Do you want it?
Lara: No, thanks. There are a ⁸ _____ biscuits.

✳ 6 Look at the picture. Write four sentences with *There's* and *There are*.

_____
_____
_____
_____

4 Ordering food

Waiter/Waitress
What would you like?
Would you like anything to drink?
Anything else?
Customer
Can I have *a vegetarian pizza*, please?
I'd like *a lemonade*, please.

1 Match 1–5 to a–e.

1 [c] What would   **a** else?
2 [ ] Can I have   **b** anything to drink?
3 [ ] Would you like   **c** you like?
4 [ ] I'd like a   **d** fish and chips, please?
5 [ ] Anything   **e** can of cola, please.

2 Match questions 1–4 to answers a–d.

1 [b] What would you like?

2 [ ] Anything else?

3 [ ] Would you like anything to drink?

4 [ ] Can I have water, please?

a Can I have a lemonade, please?

b I'd like a Hawaiian pizza, please.

c Great, thanks.

d Yes, can I have some chips, please?

3 Look at the menu. Complete the dialogues with one word in each gap.

Menu   Snack Lunches!

Cheese and ham sandwich £4.50
Fish and chips £6.00
Chicken and rice £6.50
Tuna pasta £5.00
Hot dog £2.00
Small salad £1.00
Big salad £1.50
Lemonade £1.00
Bottle of water £1.00

Waiter: What ¹ *would* you like?
Karen: I'd like fish and chips, ² _____ .
Waiter: Would you like anything to ³ _____ ?
Karen: Yes. I'd ⁴ _____ some lemonade.

Waiter: Hello. Are you ready to order?
Steve: ⁵ _____ I have the tuna pasta, please?
Waiter: Anything ⁶ _____ ?
Steve: Yes, can I have a small ⁷ _____ , please?
Waiter: Would you like anything to ⁸ _____ ?
Steve: Yes. I'd like a bottle of water.
Waiter: Great, thanks.

4 Look at the menu in Exercise 3. Write your own dialogue.

Waitress: _____
You: _____
Waitress: _____
You: _____
Waitress: _____
You: _____

Extra Online Practice

Unit 2, Video and Communication
www.myenglishlab.com

I'm Rav and I'm British

**There are some really good meals in my country.
Here are three of my favourites.**

English breakfast

This is a hot breakfast. My mum cooks it for me at the weekend. You can have different things for this breakfast, but I like some sausages, two eggs and a tomato.

Fish and chips

People usually order this meal from a restaurant. But my dad makes the best fish and chips in the world! There's always some fish in the fridge at my house because he cooks fish and chips for the whole family every Friday.

Chicken and rice

Is there any chicken on the menu at my house? No, there isn't. But there is some chicken and some rice at my aunt's house. She cooks this meal for me when I visit her. There's always a lot of food so she gives me some to take home!

1 Read the text. What is it about? Circle the correct answer.

   a My favourite meals

   b Mum's cooking

2 Read the text again. Answer the questions. Write *yes* or *no*.

   1 Is Rav from the UK? ___yes___

   2 Is an English breakfast cold? _____

   3 Does Rav like sausages? _____

   4 Does Rav order fish and chips from a restaurant? _____

   5 Does Rav's mum cook fish and chips? _____

   6 Is there any chicken and rice at his aunt's house? _____

3 Read the text again. Write the name of the meal.

   1 There are some eggs in this meal. *English breakfast*

   2 There isn't any meat in this meal. _____

   3 A lot of people order this meal. _____

   4 Rav's mum cooks this on Saturday. _____

   5 Rav's dad makes this once a week. _____

   6 Rav takes some of this meal home. _____

4 Answer the questions for you.

   1 What's your favourite meal?

   _____

   2 Who cooks it?

   _____

   3 How often do you go to restaurants?

   _____

   4 What do you usually have for breakfast?

   _____

1 Look at the photos. Complete the food words.

1 ☐ an e<u>gg</u>

2 ☐ some b_____ and h_____

3 ☐ some o_____ j_____

4 ☐ a glass of m_____

5 ☐ some s_____

6 ☐ some c_____

2 🔊 **5** Listen to the dialogue. What does Penny have for breakfast? Tick (✔) the photos in Exercise 1.

3 🔊 **5** Listen again. Circle the correct answer.

1 Penny has P.E. _____ .
  ⓐ in the morning
  b after lunch

2 She _____ for breakfast.
  a wants some cereal
  b doesn't want any cereal

3 She wants a _____ sandwich.
  a cheese
  b ham

4 She can have a glass of _____ .
  a milk
  b orange juice

5 She would like to have _____ .
  a an egg
  b two eggs

> ## so, because
>
> I'm always hungry *because* I play a lot of sport.
> I play a lot of sport *so* I'm always hungry.

4 Complete the email with *so or because*.

✉ ✕

From: Steve

Subject: What would you like to eat?

Hi Stan!

I'm very happy ¹*because* you are coming to stay at my house this weekend. Mum wants to do the shopping ²_____ she wants to know what food you like. Do you eat meat?

For breakfast I usually have milk and cereal ³_____ it is quick and easy. I also drink apple juice ⁴_____ it is my favourite. What would you like?

We can go to the beach on Saturday ⁵_____ let's take a picnic lunch. What would you like?

I love chicken and chips. Can we have that for dinner? Do you like chicken and chips too?

Bye for now!
Steve

5 Complete Stan's answer to Steve. Use *so* and *because*.

✉ ✕

From: Stan

Subject: My favourite food

Hi Steve!
I'm very happy too.
For breakfast _____
_____
For the picnic _____
_____
For dinner _____
_____

_____

Stan

Vocabulary

1 Circle the odd one out.

0 rice	pasta	(water)
1 sausages	chicken	tomatoes
2 jam	cheese	ham
3 bread	sandwiches	pancakes
4 flour	fish	tuna
5 potato	apple	lemon

☐/⑤

2 Look at the picture. Complete the sentences with one word in each gap.

0 I always take a _carton_ of orange juice to school.

1 Is there a _____ of jam in the fridge?

2 Don't forget to take a _____ of water with you to the beach.

3 Can I have a _____ of chocolate, please?

4 Can I open a new _____ of biscuits, Mum?

5 John likes a _____ of cola with his lunch.

☐/⑤

Grammar

3 Circle the correct answer.

0 I don't eat ⊝/ *a* fish because I don't like it.

1 I need *some* / *any* butter for this cake.

2 I'd like *an* / *a* banana, please.

3 We haven't got *some* / *any* eggs.

4 I think *an* / *–* orange juice is great.

5 I usually eat *–* / *an* apple in the afternoon.

☐/⑤

4 Complete the dialogues with *How much* or *How many*.

0 A: _How much_ milk is there in the fridge?

B: There isn't any milk!

1 A: _____ chocolate do you put in the cake?

B: Just one bar.

2 A: I'd like a salad, please.

B: _____ tomatoes would you like in your salad?

3 A: Matt usually eats a lot of chips.

B: _____ potatoes do we need then?

4 A: Can you buy some cream, please?

B: Yes. _____ cream do you want?

5 A: _____ water do you drink every day

B: I don't know!

☐/⑤

Communication

5 Circle the correct answer.

Waiter: What [0](would)/ *do you* like?

Daren: [1]*I'd* / *We'd* like a hot dog, please.

Waiter: [2]*Can* / *Would* you like anything to drink

Daren: Can I have a lemonade, please?

Waiter: [3]*Anything* / *Any* else?

Daren: Yes. [4]*Can* / *Would* I have a small salad please?

Waiter: Great, [5]*please* / *thanks*.

☐/⑤

Vocabulary	☐/	⑩
Grammar	☐/	⑩
Communication	☐/	⑤
Your total score		/ 25

Extra Online Practice

Unit 2, Language Revision
www.myenglishlab.com

Word blog: Food

1 My blog Look and complete.

These are my all-time favourites for breakfast.
For something that is good for you, we've got yoghurt:
apple or ¹_____ . You can put it on cereal.
Grandma's favourite is ²_____ , butter and
³_____ . ⁴_____  and eggs are for a hot
breakfast. There are pancakes with sugar and cream for
something special. We've also got chocolate
⁵_____  – oh yeah! And to drink there's
⁶_____ , tea or orange juice.

2 My photos Label the photos.

1 Monday: Italian p_ _ _ _

2 Tuesday: t_ _ _ _ _
salad

3 Wednesday: a ham
s_ _ _ _ _ _ _

4 Thursday: a strawberry
m_ _ _ _ _ _ _ _

What's your lunch today? Post your photos!

3 Get more Complete the text with the words in the box.

> bread   egg   butter   toaster

All about toast

What's toast? It's hot ¹_____ . You need
a ²_____ to cook the bread. I like toast, but …
I LOVE French toast. What's French toast? Well,
you dip your bread in an ³_____ . Then you
cook it in ⁴_____ in a frying pan. Then put
some sugar on it and it's ready.

toaster   frying pan

Get more words

> Your burger and lemonade.
> Enjoy your meal.

Look and circle the correct word.

Fun Spot

On Saturday mornings, I usually have
sausages and ¹*lemons / eggs*. I love
a hot ²*breakfast / dinner*! My mum
doesn't eat meat so she often has
³*ham / cereal* with milk. Sometimes
my dad makes pancakes for everyone.
He says that it is very ⁴*easy / difficult*
to throw a pancake in the air and
catch it, but I can't do it. We always
have a big ⁵*packet / bar* of flour and
a carton of milk in our kitchen.

Write about your school day!

Abby, 13

I live in a very small place in Wales in the UK. There are just five houses but there isn't a school. My school is in a different place so I get up at 6 a.m. That's too early! My favourite day is Wednesday because it's Computer Studies and there's strawberry ice cream in the canteen!

Bobby, 12

I live in Melbourne. It's a big city in Australia. I always get up at 8.00 a.m. School starts at 9 a.m. but I'm never late because I go with dad in the car. You can learn Chinese at my school. It's my favourite subject!

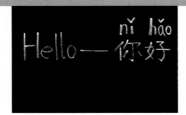

Caroline, 13

I'm English. I speak English and Spanish because I live in Spain. My school day starts at 9 a.m. and finishes at 2 p.m. Then I go home, have lunch with my granny and do my homework. Friday is my favourite day because we've got Art in the morning.

Reading and Writing

1 Read the text. Who's this? Write A (Abby), B (Bobby) or C (Caroline).

0 I live in a city. __B__

1 I get up early. ____

2 I finish school before lunch. ____

3 I speak two languages. ____

4 My favourite subject is a language. ____

5 I like strawberry ice cream. ____

6 My favourite day is Wednesday. ____

☐/⑥

2 Complete the text with the words in the box.

> dinner   don't   food   ~~like~~   make
> tuna   usually

Would you ⁰ _like_ a pizza for lunch? Yes, of course! Pizza is from Italy, but people all over the world love it. Pizza ¹_____ has cheese and tomatoes on top. People put lots of other things on it too, like chicken, ham, ²_____ fruit and vegetables.

Pizza is very popular for lunch or ³_____ in the UK. People often buy it from a supermarket so they ⁴_____ often make it. They eat it at home or with friends. Americans love pizza too. They often eat pizza in pizza restaurants. In the USA you can buy pizza for dogs and you can visit a pizza museum!

It's easy to ⁵_____ pizza at home. If you aren't good at cooking, you can buy a simple margherita pizza from a supermarket. It only has cheese and tomatoes, so you can put your favourite ⁶_____ on it!

☐/

3 Read about Jamie. Answer the questions.

I'm Jamie. My favourite subject is Science. It's on Tuesdays and Thursdays. My favourite sport is karate. It's cool! Karate Club is after school on Friday in the gym.

0 What's his name?
   His name's Jamie.

1 What's his favourite subject?
   _____

2 When is it?
   _____

3 What's his favourite sport?
   _____

4 Why is karate his favourite sport?
   _____

5 Where is Karate Club?
   _____

☐/

Listening

4 🔊 6 **Listen and tick (✔) the box.**

0 What's Monica's favourite subject?

A ✔   B ☐   C ☐

1 Where is George?

A ☐   B ☐   C ☐

2 What does Lucy have for lunch today?

A ☐   B ☐   C ☐

3 What food does mum want?

A ☐   B ☐   C ☐

4 What does Will do after school on Tuesdays?

A ☐   B ☐   C ☐

☐/4

Communication

5 Eric is in a café with his best friend and his best friend's cousin, Anabela. Eric asks Anabela some questions. Write the questions. Use the words in the box.

~~How~~ What Where Would Would

Eric: ⁰ *How do you spell you name* ?

Anabela: It's easy! You spell it A–N–A–B–E–L–A.

Eric: ¹ _____ ?

Anabela: I live in Manchester. I'm on holiday!

Eric: ² _____
_____ ?

Anabela: Anabela dot Smith at myschool dot C–O–I.

Eric: ³ _____
_____ ?

Anabela: Thanks! I'd like a lemonade.

Eric: ⁴ _____
_____ chips?

Anabela: Yes, please. I love chips!

☐/4

Reading and Writing	☐/17
Listening	☐/4
Communication	☐/4
Your total score	/ 25

3 Technology for all

3.1 Vocabulary

1 Look at the picture. What can you see? Tick (✔).

- ☐ camera ☐ headphones ☐ keyboard
- ☐ mouse ☐ printer ☐ tablet

2 Complete the sentences with the words in Exercise 1.

1 Dad takes lots of photos with his _camera_ .

2 Where's the letter G on the _____ ? Oh, I see. It's next to F.

3 Please listen to your music on your _____ ! I can't think!

4 Is there any paper in the _____ ?

5 This _____ is great. I've got films, e-books and songs on it.

6 Do you need a _____ or can you touch the screen?

3 Circle the correct answer.

My cat is tech mad! She watches ¹(TV)/ tablet every day. Bird programmes are her favourite! But she also loves my ² laptop / camera because she likes looking at the cursor – it's the little arrow on the ³ computer / screen. I move the ⁴ speakers / mouse and she watches the arrow. But when my ⁵ mobile phone / printer rings she hides! She thinks it's a dog!

4 Match the words to make phrases.

surf ①　　　　　○ online
　　　　　　　　　　　○ a friend
text ②
chat ③　　　　○ the Internet
　　　　　　　　　○ a selfie/photo
talk on ④
take ⑤　　　　　○ the phone
download ⑥　　○ a song
send ⑦　　　　○ an email

1 _surf the Internet_　　5 _____
2 _____　　　　　　6 _____
3 _____　　　　　　7 _____
4 _____

5 Complete the dialogue with one word in each gap.

A: Let's take a ¹ _selfie_ . Ready? Smile!

B: Cool! I really like your new ² _____ phone. What else do you use it for?

A: Mostly I ³ _____ my friends, ⁴ _____ the Internet and ⁵ _____ songs.

B: Can we use it to ⁶ _____ online to Terry?

A: Let's check!

I rememb
that!

6 Answer the questions for you.

1 What technology have you got?
I have _____ .

2 Which one is your favourite?
My favourite is my _____ .

3 What do you do with it?
I _____ .

Present Continuous affirmative and negative

+	–
I'm talking.	I'm not talking.
You're talking.	You aren't talking.
He/She/It's talking.	He/She/It isn't talking.
We/You/They're talking.	We/You/They aren't talking.

1 Complete the sentences with *am*, *are* or *is*.

1 Mum __is__ working today.
2 They _____ chatting online at the moment.
3 He _____ taking a photo of a famous person.
4 We _____ watching a film on TV.
5 I _____ wearing my tracksuit because we have P.E.
6 You _____ wearing a nice T-shirt. Is it new?

2 Write the opposite.

1 He's reading a book.
   He isn't reading a book.
2 I'm downloading a song.
   _____
3 They're doing their homework.
   _____
4 She isn't texting a friend.
   _____
5 You're sitting in my seat.
   _____
6 We aren't taking a selfie.
   _____

LOOK!

look + ing = looking
take + ing = taking
sit + t + ing = sitting

Complete the spelling table.

~~ask~~ chat dance have run
stop surf wait write

look – looking	take – taking	sit – sitting
asking	_____	_____
_____	_____	_____
_____	_____	_____

4 Complete the text with the correct forms of the Present Continuous.

Amy, Tom and Elena are at a café. Amy
¹ *is taking* (take) a selfie. She ² _____
(not use) her mobile phone. It's Tom's phone.
They ³ _____ (smile). They ⁴ _____
(not eat) anything. Tom ⁵ _____ (hold)
a ball with an autograph.

✳ 5 Write affirmative and negative sentences. Use the correct form of the verbs.

1 shop / cook
   They're shopping at the supermarket.
   They aren't cooking dinner.

2 do / watch
   He _____ .
   _____
   _____

3 play / listen
   _____
   _____
   _____
   _____

4 text / eat
   _____
   _____
   _____
   _____

Extra Online Practice

Unit 3, Video and Grammar
www.myenglishlab.com

Present Continuous questions and short answers

?	Short answers
Am I coming?	Yes, I am. / No, I'm not.
Are you coming?	Yes, you are. / No, you aren't.
Is he/she/it coming?	Yes, he/she/it is. / No, he/she/it isn't.
Are we/you/they coming?	Yes, we/you/they are. / No, we/you/they aren't.

What are you doing?
Where's it going?
Why are they running?

1 Complete the questions with *am*, *are*, or *is*.

Carla: Hi Rocco. ¹ _Are_ you playing with Big Al?
Rocco: No, I'm not. ² _____ you playing with Big Al?
Carla: No, I'm not! Where is he? What ³ _____ Big Al doing?
Rocco: I don't know. ⁴ _____ he answering his phone?
Carla: No, he isn't!

Big Al: Hi Carla. What ⁵ _____ you doing? ⁶ _____ we playing a game?
Carla: No, Big Al. I'm looking for you. I'm worried.

2 Complete the short answers.

1 Are you sending an email?   Yes, I _am_ .
2 Is he doing his homework?   Yes, he ____ .
3 Is she listening to music?   No, she ____ .
4 Are you having lunch?   Yes, we ____ .
5 Are they wearing hats?   No, they ____ .
6 Am I dreaming?   No, you ____ .

✳ **3** Write questions. Then answer them for you.

1 you / text a friend now
  Are you texting a friend now?
  _____

2 you / send an email now
  _____
  _____

3 your friend / text you now
  _____
  _____

4 your friends / do their homework now
  _____
  _____

5 what / you / wear now
  _____
  _____

4 **Vocabulary** How do they feel? Complete the sentences with the words in the box. There is one extra word.

angry	bored	happy	sad
scared	~~tired~~	worried	

1 It's _tired_ .   2 He's _____ .

3 He's _____ .   4 They're _____

5 They're _____ .   6 It's _____ .

🔊 **7 Talking on the phone**

Hello, it's *Elena* here.
Can I speak to *Amy*, please?
Just one moment. / Just a minute. / Hang on.
It's *Elena* for you.
I'm afraid *he's / she's* out.
Bye. / See you soon. / See you later.

1 Circle the correct answer.

1 A: Hello. Can I speak to Kay, please?
   B: _____
   ⓐ Just a minute.
   b See you later.

2 A: It's Greg here. Can I speak to Steve, please?
   B: _____
   a I'm afraid she's out.
   b I'm afraid he's out.

3 A: Hello Mrs Davies. It's Bob here. Can I speak to Dan, please?
   B: _____
   a Hang on, Dan.
   b Yes, just a moment.

4 A: Hi Martha. It's Lucas here. What are you doing?
   B: _____
   a I'm watching TV. What about you?
   b Bye! See you soon.

5 A: See you in 30 minutes.
   B: _____
   a OK. Just a minute.
   b OK. See you later.

Put the dialogue in the correct order.

a ☐ I'm watching TV. What about you, Neil?
b ☐ Yes, Neil. Just a minute. Vicky, it's for you!
c ☐1 Hello Mrs Green. It's Neil here. Can I speak to Vicky?
d ☐ Nothing. Do you want to go swimming at five, Vicky?
e ☐ Hi Vicky. What are you doing?
f ☐ Bye! See you later.
g ☐ Yes. Great idea. See you soon.

3 Complete the dialogues with one word in each gap.

Janet: ¹ _Hello_ . It's Janet ² _____ . Can I
          ³ _____ to Billy, please?
Mrs Dee: ⁴ _____ Janet. ⁵ _____ on. Billy, it's
          ⁶ _____ you!

Janet: Hi Billy. ⁷ _____ are you doing at the
        ⁸ _____ ?
Billy: Nothing. What ⁹ _____ you?
Janet: ¹⁰ _____ bored. Do you want to go to the cinema?
Billy: Great ¹¹ _____ ! See you in ten minutes.
Janet: Bye. See you ¹² _____ .

4 Complete this dialogue with your own ideas.

Your friend: Hello, it's ¹ _____ . Can I
             ² _____ , please?
Your dad: Hello, ³ _____ . Just ⁴ _____ .
Your friend: Hi ⁵ _____ . What ⁶ _____ at the moment?
You: Nothing. What about you?
Your friend: I'm bored. Do you want to ⁷ _____ ?
You: Great idea. See ⁸ _____ .

Extra Online Practice

Unit 3, Video and Communication
www.myenglishlab.com

TECH TED

Tech Ted is interviewing Dave Fernandez. Dave is a young technology blogger and student at North Street Secondary School.

Tech Ted: Hi Dave. I can see some photos on the screen. What are you doing in this photo?

Dave: Hi Ted. In this photo I'm talking to some parents from my school.

Tech Ted: What are you talking about?

Dave: I'm asking the parents for help. We need computers for my school.

Tech Ted: What's wrong with computers at your school?

Dave: A lot of our computers are old and slow. My friend Hunter knows a lot about computers and sometimes he can fix them. But when they stop working, we can't do Computer Studies lessons.

Tech Ted: How can the parents help?

Dave: Well, their families can give their old computers to my school. You know, computers or tablets they don't use. But ones that work of course.

Tech Ted: Do parents help?

Dave: Yes! We have four computers and two tablets already. It's amazing.

Tech Ted: That's brilliant. Good luck with your Computer Studies lessons!

Dave: Thanks!

1 Read the interview. Who is Dave? _____

2 Read the interview again. Answer *yes* or *no*.

1 Are there some photos on Dave's screen? *yes*
2 Is he talking to friends in the photo? ____
3 Is he asking people for help in the photo? ____
4 Can Dave do Computer Studies at school? ____
5 Does he want new computers for his school? ____
6 Have they got some computers and tablets? ____

3 Read the text again. Answer the questions.

1 Who is Tech Ted interviewing?

_____

2 Who is Dave talking to in the photo?

_____

3 What does his school need?

_____

4 What can families do to help?

_____

4 **Vocabulary** Complete the sentences wit the correct prepositions.

1 He's worried _about_ the computer studies lessons.
2 He's interested _____ technology.
3 She's good _____ playing computer games.
4 Are you scared _____ aliens?
5 I'm really excited _____ my new tablet
6 Grandpa is bad _____ using my mobi phone.

1 🔊 8 Listen to the dialogue. What is Harry's and Lily's favourite technology item? Tick (✔).

Harry

Lily

2 🔊 8 Listen again. Complete the sentences with one word in each gap.

1 Harry watches __films__ on TV and on his tablet.

2 Harry likes _____ videos.

3 Lily chats _____ a lot with her friends.

4 Lily also likes _____ the Internet.

5 Lily takes her _____ everywhere.

3 🔊 8 Who says what? Match 1–5 to Harry or Lily. Then listen again and check.

Harry: ☐1☐ ☐
Lily: ☐ ☐ ☐

1 I've got a TV. I've also got a tablet.

2 I've got a mobile phone and I've got a laptop too.

3 I download videos to my tablet.

4 I also like surfing the Internet.

5 I can also put it in my jacket.

---

also and too

1 **Too** usually comes at the end of a sentence.

2 **Also** usually comes before the verb.

I listen to music on my CDs. I listen to music on my phone **too**.

I use the computer to do my homework. I **also** use it to talk to my grandparents.

4 Complete the text with *also* or *too*.

My favourite technology item

My name is Lily. I love technology. I've got a laptop. I've ¹ __also__ got a mobile phone. I chat online to my friends on my phone. I surf the Internet on my phone ² _____ . I play games on my laptop and I do my homework on my laptop ³ _____ .

My friend Harry ⁴ _____ likes technology. He's got a TV and a tablet ⁵ _____ . He downloads videos to his tablet.

5 Complete the notes with your own ideas.

My technology items: ¹ _____ and ² _____
I use item 1 to _____ .
I use item 2 to _____ .
My friend's technology items: ¹ _____ and
² _____
My friend uses _____ to _____

6 Now write about your favourite technology item. Use your ideas from Exercise 5, *also* and *too*.

My favourite technology item

My name is _____ . *I've got* _____

_____

_____

_____

My friend

_____

_____

_____

Vocabulary

1 Circle the correct answer.

0 Is there any paper in the *speakers /(printer)*?

1 Turn on the *camera / headphones* so I can see you.

2 Let's watch a film on *the keyboard / TV*.

3 I *worry about / am good at* Computer Studies. I always get 20/20 in the test.

4 Are you *scared of / bad at* this film? Don't watch it then!

5 I like your *mouse / tablet*. The screen is very clear. ☐/⑤

2 Look at the pictures. Complete the sentences with one word in each gap.

 0 Dad's talking on the *phone* with his brother.

 1 How often do you _____ your friend?

 2 Let's _____ a selfie.

 **3** I sometimes _____ the Internet in the evening.

 **4** We often chat _____ because we've got cameras on our computers.

 5 I _____ songs to my phone. ☐/⑤

Grammar

3 Complete the sentences with the verb in the Present Continuous.

0 I *am listening* (listen) to my favourite song.

1 He _____ (send) an email.

2 She _____ (not do) her homework.

3 We _____ (wear) black tracksuits.

4 They _____ (not have) lunch.

5 I _____ (run) really fast! ☐/⑤

4 Complete the questions and short answers.

0 A: *Are you talking* (you/talk) on the phone?
  B: No, I'm not.

1 A: _____ (she/make) a cake?
  B: Yes, she is.

2 A: Are you sending an email?
  B: ✔ _____

3 A: _____ (Tom/sit) in the café?
  B: Yes, he is.

4 A: Are you and your sister eating ice cream?
  B: ✗ _____

5 A: _____ (your parents/watch) the news?
  B: Yes, they are. ☐/⑤

Communication

5 Complete the dialogue with one word in each gap.

Tina: ⁰ *Hello* , Mrs Brown. It's Tina ¹ _____ Can I ² _____ to Matt, please?

Mrs Brown: I'm ³ _____ he isn't in. No, hang on, there he is. He's coming home now. I can see him in the garden. ⁴ _____ a moment, Tina.

Tina: Thank you. Bye, Mrs Brown.

Mrs Brown: ⁵ _____ you soon, dear. Matt, it's Tina.

☐/⑤

Vocabulary	☐/⑩
Grammar	☐/⑩
Communication	☐/⑤
Your total score	/ 25

 **Extra Online Practice**

Unit 3, Language Revision
www.myenglishlab.com

Read Maria's blog to find out about technology.

Word blog: Technology

1 My photos Complete the words.

In my family, we love technology.

On my mum'd desk, there's a l_ _ _ _ _ _, a m_ _ _ _ _ p_ _ _ _ and a c_ _ _ _ _.

My brother has got a big s_ _ _ _ _, a k_ _ _ _ _ _ _, s_ _ _ _ _ _ _ and a m_ _ _ _.

2 Get more We often use short words when we chat. What are the short forms?

1 Internet	→	Net
2 television	→	
3 photograph	→	
4 mobile phone	→	
5 electronic book	→	
6 telephone	→	

3 My friends Read the comments and complete the words.

Danny 1 I love surfing the l_ _ _ _ _!
And I d_ _ _ _ _ songs to my phone.

Trisha 2 I t_ _ _ _ _ selfies all the time!
And I t_ _ _ _ _ my friends every day.

Bob 3 I c_ _ _ _ _ online with my cousins in Scotland. And I s_ _ _ _ _ emails to my grandpa in Canada!

Joe 4 What do I do? I talk all the time on the p_ _ _ _ _!

Get more words

Save my number so we can stay in touch.

How many of the words on the right can you find in the word search?

T	C	M	U	S	T	E	X	T	H	S
E	O	E	W	C	A	G	G	A	R	O
C	N	B	T	R	K	A	E	B	E	N
H	S	L	L	E	E	M	C	L	N	G
N	O	O	A	E	T	E	L	E	Q	W
O	L	G	F	N	G	O	N	T	B	A
L	E	M	O	U	S	E	S	U	R	F
O	N	O	D	O	W	N	L	O	A	D
G	R	D	R	H	L	A	P	T	O	P
Y	E	M	A	I	L	V	I	D	E	O

Fun Spot

- [ ] blog
- [ ] camera
- [ ] console
- [ ] download
- [ ] email
- [ ] game
- [ ] laptop
- [ ] mouse
- [ ] screen
- [ ] selfie
- [ ] simulator
- [ ] song
- [ ] speakers
- [ ] surf
- [ ] tablet
- [ ] technology
- [ ] text
- [ ] video

4 Big world

4.1 Vocabulary

Beautiful Islands

1 **Label the photos with the words in the box.**

> beach   forest   lake   mountain
> ~~sea~~   waterfall

1 ___sea___   4 _____
2 _____   5 _____
3 _____   6 _____

2 **Look at the pictures and complete words 1–6.**

1   i _s_ _l_ _a_ n d

2   f _ _ _ _ t

3   v _ _ _ _ _ o

4   b _ _ _ h

5   m _ _ _ _ _ _ n

6   d _ _ _ _ t

3 **Match words a–f to definitions 1–6.**

1 [b] There are a lot of trees.
2 [   ] There aren't any plants because it's too hot.
3 [   ] This is a mountain but it hasn't got a top.
4 [   ] People live in this big place.
5 [   ] People live in this small place.
6 [   ] There is sand next to the sea.

a desert   c town   e beach
b forest   d volcano   f city

4 **Read and circle the correct answer.**

I live in Greece. There are ¹(forests) / *deserts* with lots of trees and there are lots of ² *islands* / *waterfalls* in the sea. I live in a small ³ *beach* / *town*. In the holidays, I sometimes stay with my uncle in the big ⁴ *city* / *river*. In winter, we always go skiing in the ⁵ *mountains* / *lake*. In summer, we go to an island. I like swimming in the ⁶ *volcano* / *sea*.

I rememb that!

5 **Complete the table with your own ideas.**

Holiday places	Winter or summer?	Activities you can do there?	How often do you go there?
sea or lake			
forest			
mountain			
town or city			

Comparative adjectives

Adjective	Comparative
Short adjectives	
cold	colder
nice	nicer
easy	easier
big	bigger
Long adjectives	
exciting	more exciting
Irregular adjectives	
good	better
bad	worse

That wall is lower.
Kayaking is more exciting than cycling.

Match 1–6 to a–f.

1 [c] I'm taller than
2 [ ] Kayaking is more
3 [ ] Hamburgers are better than
4 [ ] Walking is slower than
5 [ ] Winter weather is worse than
6 [ ] Geography books are more

a hot dogs.
b interesting than Maths books.
c my friend.
d summer weather.
e running.
f exciting than cycling.

Vocabulary Complete the adjectives.

| cit | cult | ffi | ge | gh | ~~pen~~ |
| rous | ~~sive~~ | ing |

1 ex + _pen_ + _sive_ = _expensive_

2 hi + ___ = _____

3 dan + ___ + ___ = _____

4 di + ___ + ___ = _____

5 ex + ___ + ___ = _____

3 Complete the dialogue with the comparative form of the adjective.

Tom: Let's go swimming in the lake. The water today is ¹ _hotter_ (hot) than yesterday.

Lucas: No. Let's go kayaking. It's ² _____ _____ (exciting) than swimming.

Tom: OK. Let's get a kayak for two. Two people are ³ _____ (fast) than one person.

Lucas: OK. And my arms are ⁴ _____ (long) than your arms so I can help you.

Tom: What? That's not true! My arms aren't ⁵ _____ (short) than yours!

Lucas: Yes, they are. And I'm a ⁶ _____ (good) swimmer than you.

Tom: No, you aren't. You are a ⁷ _____ (bad) swimmer than me!

4 Write the opposites. Use the words in brackets.

1 Olga is taller than Mark. (short)
   Mark is shorter than Olga.

2 Maths is more boring than Science. (interesting)
   _____

3 My dog is smaller than your cat. (big)
   _____

4 The English test is easier than the French test. (difficult)
   _____

5 Skateboarding is more dangerous than running. (safe)
   _____

✱ 5 Complete the words.

1 The water in this bottle is _colder_ than the Arctic!
2 Sailing is m_____ dangerous than cycling.
3 I'm shorter t_____ my brother.
4 This bad painting is w_____ than that good painting.
5 I can't do my homework. It's more d_____ than the lesson.
6 He's a better runner t_____ you.

Extra Online Practice

Unit 4, Video and Grammar
www.myenglishlab.com

Superlative adjectives

Adjective	Comparative	Superlative
Short adjectives		
tall	taller	the tallest
strong	stronger	the strongest
big	bigger	the biggest
funny	funnier	the funniest
Long adjectives		
dangerous	more dangerous	the most dangerous
Irregular adjectives		
good	better	the best
bad	worse	the worst

He's the funniest.
They're the most dangerous animals in the world.

1 Vocabulary Complete the sentences with the words in the box. There is one extra word.

> beautiful   fast   friendly   funny   intelligent
> kind   ~~strong~~

1 Elephants are _strong_ animals.
2 Thank you for helping me. You are a _____ person.
3 This is a very _____ sports car. It can do 150 km an hour!
4 He always gets 100% in tests because he is _____ .
5 That clown has a red nose. It's _____ .
6 My _____ dog likes playing with my friends in the park.

2 Look at the pictures. Complete the sentences with the superlative form of the adjectives in the box.

> small   funny   tall

1 The giraffe is _the tallest_ .
2 The hippo is _____ .
3 The elephant is _____ .

> friendly   dangerous
> intelligent

4 The lion _____ .
5 The dog _____ .
6 The monkey _____
_____ .

3 Look at the pictures and circle the corr____ answer.

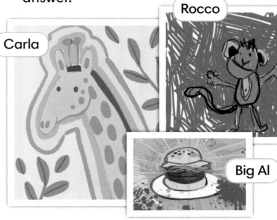

Rocco

Carla

Big Al

1 Rocco's painting is (bigger than)/ the biggest Big Al's painting, but Carla's painting is bigger / the biggest of all.
2 Big Al's picture and Carla's picture are better than / the best Rocco's picture. His painting isn't good! I think it is worse than / the worst.
3 I think Big Al is funnier than / the funniest artist of all. His picture is more interesting the most interesting than Carla's picture.

✱ 4 Complete the text with one word in each gap.

Tigers are bigger [1] _than_ pet cats. They are also [2] _____ dangerous than pet cats. They eat meat. They are faster [3] _____ many animals so they can catch them. I think tigers are [4] _____ most beautiful cats in the world. They've got the nicest colours [5] _____ all the cats. They've also got the best faces of [6] _____ .

✱ 5 Write sentences about animals. Use the words below and your own ideas.

1 nicer than
Giraffes are nicer than monkeys.
2 smaller than
_____
3 more intelligent than
_____
4 the funniest
_____
5 the most beautiful
_____

4.4

🔊 9 Opinions

Asking for opinions

What's your favourite film?

What about you?

What do you think of *cartoons*?

Giving opinions

My favourite film is *Action Team*.

I think *Electro Max* is *more exciting*.

In my opinion, they are *a bit silly*.

You're right. They are *silly*.

1 Put the words in the correct order to make sentences.

1 your What's subject favourite ?

What's your favourite subject?

2 opinion In bit , a my it's silly .

_____

3 about you What , Kim ?

_____

4 think I exciting are that cartoons more .

_____

5 do think of What adventure stories you ?

_____

2 Complete the dialogue with one word in each gap.

Patty: What's your ¹ *favourite* book, Billy?

Billy: ² _____ favourite book is *Harry Potter and the Philosopher's Stone*.

Patty: What do you think ³ _____ adventure stories?

Billy: I ⁴ _____ adventure stories are great. ⁵ _____ about you, Patty?

Patty: In my ⁶ _____ , funny stories are better than adventure stories.

Bill: Well, Harry Potter books are adventure stories and they are funny too.

Patty: You're ⁷ _____ .

3 Circle the correct answer.

1 What do you think of cartoons?

   (a) I think they're funny.

   b That's true.

2 What about you?

   a I prefer *Transformers*.

   b I often watch a film.

3 In my opinion, *Frozen* is a great film.

   a I think so.

   b You're right.

4 I think action films are better than cartoons.

   a My favourite cartoon is *Frozen*.

   b In my opinion, cartoons are better.

5 Do you like cartoons or action films?

   a Cartoons. I think they are funnier than action films.

   b I don't like watching cartoons.

4 Read the texts. Then complete the table.

Tina: I like cartoons. I don't like action films. My favourite film is *Minions*. I think it is funnier than an action film.

Gary: I don't like cartoons. I like action films. My favourite film is *Transformers*. I think it is more exciting than a cartoon.

	Cartoons or action films?	Favourite film	Why?
Tina	*cartoons*		
Gary			

5 Look at Exercise 4. Complete the dialogue.

Tina: What's your favourite film?

Gary: My _____ .

     What about you?

Tina: My _____ .

Gary: What do you think of _____ ?

Tina: I think cartoons _____ .

     What do you think?

Gary: In my _____ ,

     action films _____ .

Extra Online Practice

Unit 4, Video and Communication
www.myenglishlab.com

Friday 24th May: School Records Competition

What do you think of world records? In my opinion, they are fun and interesting. Well, we have a School Records Competition every year. It is the funniest day of the year! Everyone can join the fun!

These are some records to beat:

> **Thomas Baker:** He's the fastest runner. 100m in 14.4 seconds!

> **Katie Lancer:** She's the most intelligent student. 19/20 questions correct in 5 minutes.

> **Mrs Price (our Maths teacher!):** Her pizza is the longest of all: 80 centimetres long!

> **Daniella (Mr Nunn's pet cat!):** She's the most beautiful pet of all. Bring your photos, not your pets!

Are you faster, taller, more intelligent or maybe funnier than your classmates?

Then come to the School Records Competition and be the best!

Check out the after school clubs website for all the records you can try. There are a lot of them!

Contact me: Gordon Butler for forms.

1 Read the text. What is the text about? Tick (✔).

A  B  C  D

2 Read the text again and write the names.

Who …

1 is the fastest runner? _Thomas Baker_
2 has the competition forms? _____
3 is the cleverest person? _____
4 has the most beautiful pet? _____
5 can make the longest pizza? _____

3 Read the text again. Answer the questions.

1 What's the name of the competition?
School Records Competition
2 When is the competition? _____
3 What does Gordon think of world records?
_____
4 Who can join the fun? _____
5 Where can you find all the records?
_____
6 How many records are there to try?
_____

LOOK!

It's 979 metres high.
It's 28 centimetres long.
It's 828 metres tall.
He's / She's 185 years old.

4 Match 1–5 to a–e.

1 [b] My parents
2 [ ] The Eiffel tower
3 [ ] My baby sister
4 [ ] My dad
5 [ ] This ruler

a is 12 months old.
b are 42 years old.
c is 324 metres high.
d is 30 centimetres long.
e is 1 metre 80 centimetres tall.

🔊 10 **Listen and match people 1–4 to their best friends and the photos.**

Dave
Mary
Zach
Fiona

1 Lenny
2 Bella
3 Fred
4 Diana

🔊 10 **Listen again. Complete the sentences with the words in the box.**

| beautiful | best | fastest | funny | good |
| intelligent | ~~older~~ | smaller | | |

1 Zach is _older_ than Lenny.
2 Lenny thinks that Zach is _____ .
3 Fiona is _____ than Bella.
4 Fiona is the most _____ animal.
5 Dave is the _____ runner in the family.
6 Dave is the _____ friend in the world.
7 Mary is the most _____ girl in the class.
8 Diana thinks that Mary is a _____ teacher.

Paragraphs

A paragraph is a part of a text. It's about one main idea. Remember to divide your text into paragraphs!

Read Lenny's description of his best friend. Put the paragraphs in the correct order.

My best friend by Lenny

A ☐
We both like cycling. We go cycling in the mountains. We both like playing football, but Zach is faster than I am! We also like playing basketball.

B ☐
My best friend is called Zach. He's a lot of fun. We spend a lot of time together. In some ways we are similar, but in other ways we are different.

C ☐
But we are also different. I am 12, but Zach is 15. Zach likes pizza, but I like hamburgers. Zach is a worse Maths student, but he's a better Art student. He's a great friend.

4 **Complete the table for Lenny and Zach.**

Similar	We both like _cycling_, _____ and _____ .	
	Lenny	**Zach**
Different	Age: ____	Age: ____
	Food: ____	Food: ____
	Good at: ____	Good at: ____

5 **Now write Zach's description of Lenny.**

My best friend by Zach
My best friend is called _____
_____
_____
_____
We _____
_____
_____
_____
But _____
_____
_____
_____

Vocabulary

1 Circle the correct answer.

0 (sea)/ river   1 forest / city

2 volcano / island   3 desert / waterfall

4 town / mountain   5 lake / beach

☐/⑤

2 Complete the sentences with the words in the box. There are two extra words.

> cheap difficult easy ~~exciting~~
> expensive fast friendly safe

0 Geography trips aren't boring. They're
exciting .
1 Be careful. That dog isn't _____ .
2 I can't do my homework. It's _____ .
3 He is a _____ runner.
4 I can't buy this watch because it's very
_____ .
5 My bike isn't dangerous. It's _____ .

☐/⑤

Grammar

3 Complete the sentences with the comparative form of the adjective and *than*.

0 My feet are _bigger_ _than_ (big) your feet!
1 This test is _____ _____ (easy) the last test.
2 I think it's _____ _____ _____ (difficult) the last te
3 My brother is _____ _____ (good) me at Maths!
4 This car is _____ _____ _____ (expensive) that on
5 Today is _____ _____ (hot) yesterday.

☐/

4 Write sentences using the superlative form of the adjective.

0 this / be / high / mountain in my country
This is the highest mountain in my country.
1 this pizza / be / cheap / meal
_____
2 this / be / good / holiday of all
_____
3 this / be / bad / ice cream
_____
4 my sister / be / beautiful / person in my family
_____
5 you / be / intelligent / student in my class
_____

☐/

Communication

5 Circle the correct answer.

Lucas: 0 What /(What's) your favourite film?
Amy: My 1 favourite is / favourite film is Frozen. What
       2 do / about you?
Lucas: I like Shrek. What do you 3 thinking / think of
       going to the cinema?
Amy: 4 In / On my opinion, it's great.
Lucas: You're 5 right / true. Going to the cinema is grea

☐/

> Vocabulary ☐/⑩
> Grammar ☐/⑩
> Communication ☐/⑤
> **Your total score** / 25

Extra Online Practice
Unit 4, Language Revision
www.myenglishlab.com

Word blog: Big, bigger, the biggest!

1 My photos Circle the correct answer.

1 I like big *mountains / cities / islands*.

2 I like activities on the *sea / river / beach*.

3 We always ride bikes in the *forest / city / volcano*.

4 I love activities on the *town / lake / desert*.

2 About me Complete the missing letters.

I like city holidays. Cities are not ¹b_r_ng at all. They are ²exc_t_ng places. They are sometimes ³exp_ns_v_ , so you need money. But you can find ⁴ch_ _p places to eat burgers and pizzas. In many cities there are ⁵b_ _ _ t_f_l parks. Some cities are ⁶d_ng_r_ _s because there are lots of ⁷f_st cars. But most cities have got buses, so it is ⁸_ _sy to get to places. People are usually ⁹fr_ _ndly and ¹⁰k_nd to tourists. I always have fun in a city holiday.

3 Get more Match pictures 1–5 to the words.

kayaking
jumping with a parachute
fishing
climbing
sailing

Get more words

Home is the best place. Home sweet home.

Look at the map. Complete the sentences.

	1	2	3
A			
B			
C			

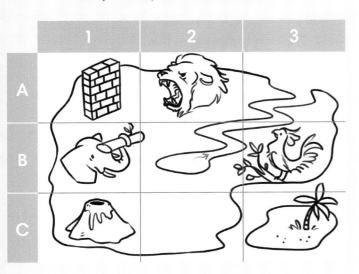

1 There is a h_____ w_____ in A1 .

2 There is a s_____ e_____ in B1 .

3 A r_____ goes from B2 to A3 .

4 The l_____ in A2 is d_____ .

5 There is a v_____ in C1 .

6 The i_____ in C3 is s_____ .

7 There is a b_____ b_____ in B3 .

Fun Spot

TECHNOLOGY REPORT

Read about favourite technology we have at home!

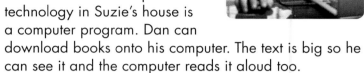

Micky Bailey's parents have got a ... robot! They're very excited about it. It's a kitchen robot and it makes dinner for Micky's family every day. It's very good at cooking! Micky's mum and dad are really happy. Now they don't need to cook dinner so now they've got more time. All they need to do is go shopping!

David Smith's new puppy, Attila, is friendly and intelligent. David is worried about Attila because he sometimes gets lost. Like all dogs in the UK, Attila has got a microchip so the police know his name and address. The microchip isn't new technology but it's David's favourite!

Suzie Highton's brother Dan can't see very well. He can't see text in books. The most important technology in Suzie's house is a computer program. Dan can download books onto his computer. The text is big so he can see it and the computer reads it aloud too.

Reading and Writing

1 Read the texts. Complete the sentences with one or two words in each gap.

0 Micky's parents are _very excited_ about their new robot.

1 The robot is _____ cooking.

2 Attila is David's _____ .

3 David is _____ Attila because he sometimes gets lost.

4 David's favourite technology is Attila's _____ .

5 Suzie Highton's brother can't _____ very well.

6 Dan can see text on his computer because it's _____ .

2 Look at the picture. Complete the sentences 1–3 and answer the questions 4–6.

0 The boy with the tablet feels _scared_ .

00 What's the woman doing? _reading a book_

1 The dog is playing in the _____ .

2 The blue boat is bigger than _____ .

3 The yellow boat is the _____ .

4 What is the girl doing?

_____

5 What's the girl wearing?

_____

6 What's the woman wearing?

_____

◯/⑥   ◯/◯

3 Read and answer the questions.

Shark City

Price: **£22**

August 2017

Help friendly Simon shark find his family!

Easy √

Volcano Disaster!

Price: **£12**

March 2015

Catch the magic mouse before the volcano explodes!

Easy √ √ √

Desert Adventure

Price: **£18**

September 2017

Find the road to the Secret City!

Easy √ √

0 What are the Shark City, Volcano Disaster and Desert Adventure? *They are computer games.*

1 What's the shark doing?

_____

2 What's the girl doing?

_____

3 Which game is the most expensive?

_____

4 Is Desert Adventure more difficult than Volcano Disaster?

_____

5 Which is the newest game?

_____

◯/⑤

Listening

🔊 **11** Listen and write.

Sophie's homework

Sophie is doing her: *Geography* homework

Studying: mountains, lakes and _____

Ben Nevis, Scotland: the _____ mountain in the UK

Windermere: _____ kilometres long

Volcanoes: sometimes _____

◯/④

Communication

5 Read the sentences and circle the best answer.

0 **Ben:** Are you busy?

  May: **A** No, I'm doing my homework.

   B Yes, it's busy.

   Ⓒ Yes, I'm downloading music.

1 **Ben:** Let's go to the cinema!

  May: **A** OK. Tickets are cheap today.

   B You're right, it's boring.

   C OK. It's on TV.

2 **Ben:** What do you think of Star Trek?

  May: **A** I'm worried about it.

   B I think it's amazing!

   C Well done!

3 **Ben:** What time is the film?

  May: **A** It's at 5 p.m.

   B We can walk.

   C Yes, it is.

4 **Ben:** Let's meet at my house.

  May: **A** I like your house.

   B What's my address?

   C OK, see you later.

◯/④

Reading and Writing	◯/⑰
Listening	◯/④
Communication	◯/④
Your total score	/ 25

Around town

5.1 Vocabulary

1 Label places 1–6 with the words in the box.

> café   cinema   hospital   hotel
> ~~restaurant~~   supermarket

1 *restaurant*   3 _____   5 _____
2 _____   4 _____   6 _____

2 Circle the correct answer.

1 I want to get some eggs and flour from the *café* / *(supermarket)*.
2 Let's go to the *bank* / *cinema* to get some money.
3 This is a nice *shop* / *library*. I love the clothes they sell.
4 Who wants to see an Egyptian mummy at the *hotel* / *museum*?
5 There's a football match on Saturday at the *theatre* / *stadium*.
6 Can we have a picnic in the *park* / *hospital* please, Mum?

3 Where's Rex? Label the pictures with the prepositions in the box.

> behind   ~~between~~   in front of
> next to   opposite

1 *between*   2 _____   3 _____

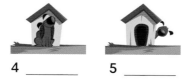

4 _____   5 _____

4 Look at the map and complete the dialogue with the prepositions in the box.

> behind   between   in front of   ~~next to~~   opposite

NORTH STREET   *SOUTH STREET*   PARK

A: Where's the café? I'd like a cup of coffee.
B: It's ¹*next to* my favourite clothes shop in North Street. But I haven't got any money, so let's go to the bank first. It's ² _____ the library and the Italian restaurant.
A: I know, it's near the hotel in South Street. There is a lovely garden ³ _____ the hotel and there is a park ⁴ _____ it.
B: Yes. The supermarket is ⁵ _____ the café, so we can get some food for a picnic …
A: … and have lunch in the park. Good idea.

I remember that!

5 Match places 1–8 to words a–h. Can you add another word for each place?

1 [a] restaurant   a waiter *lunch*
2 [ ] cinema   b eggs _____
3 [ ] library   c popcorn _____
4 [ ] bank   d hot chocolate _____
5 [ ] stadium   e trees _____
6 [ ] café   f sport _____
7 [ ] park   g £20 _____
8 [ ] supermarket h comics _____

Past Simple *to be* affirmative and negative

+	−
I was at the cinema.	I wasn't at the park.
You were at the cinema.	You weren't at the park.
He/She/It was at the cinema.	He/She/It wasn't at the park.
We/You/They were at the cinema.	We/You/They weren't at the park.
there was / were	*there wasn't / weren't*
There was a problem.	There wasn't a problem.
There were some buses.	There weren't any buses.

wasn't = was not   weren't = were not

Circle the correct answer.

1 I (was) / were at the shops.
2 Mum and Dad *was / were* at work.
3 We *was / were* at school.
4 Sam *wasn't / weren't* at home.
5 My grandparents *wasn't / weren't* at the theatre.
6 Anna *were / was* at school yesterday.
7 There *was / were* some people at the bank.
8 These shoes *weren't / wasn't* expensive.

Complete the dialogue with *was, wasn't, were* or *weren't*.

 Tom    Lucas

Lucas: Tell me about the film. I ¹ *was* late. I ² _____ there, remember?

Tom: I remember! Amy and Elena ³ _____ worried about you.

Lucas: I know. Sorry!

Tom: Well, it ⁴ _____ a really good film. I'm sad you ⁵ _____ there. The popcorn ⁶ _____ great, too.

Lucas: Oh no! I love popcorn.

LOOK!

yesterday   last night/week/month/year
last Monday/May   in 2014

3 Match the dates to the words in the box.

last month   last night   last Saturday
last year   yesterday

Today is **8** It's Tuesday.
FEBRUARY

1 7 February = _yesterday_
2 7 February at 8 p.m. = _____
3 8 January = _____
4 8 December = _____
5 5 February = _____

4 Read Elena's texts and write sentences.

Elena: Friday   **Mum:**

Lucas isn't well.   ☹

The History test = easy!   ☺

Saturday
We are at the cinema. Where is Lucas?   I don't know.

8 pm: at Amy's house.   OK. Is there food?

Some nice hot dogs. ☺

1 Friday / Lucas not well
Last Friday Lucas wasn't well.

2 History test / easy
_____

3 Last Saturday / Lucas / not at the cinema
_____

4 at 8 p.m. / the friends / Amy's house
_____

5 there / some nice hot dogs
_____

⋆5 Complete the sentences using your own ideas.

1 I _____ last Monday.
2 I _____ yesterday.
3 In 2017, my favourite film _____ .

Extra Online Practice

Unit 5, Video and Grammar
www.myenglishlab.com

45

Past Simple *to be* questions and short answers

?	Short answers
Was I at the park?	Yes, I was. / No, I wasn't.
Were you at the park?	Yes, you were. / No, you weren't.
Was he/she/it at the park?	Yes, he/she/it was. / No, he/she/it wasn't.
Were we/you/they at the park?	Yes, we/you/they were. / No, we/you/they weren't.

there was / there were	
Was there a pizza in the fridge?	Yes, there was. / No, there wasn't.
Were there (any) muffins in the fridge?	Yes, there were. / No, there weren't.

1 Circle the correct answer.

1 **A:** Were you at the bank?
   B: Yes, I (was) / wasn't.

2 **A:** Was Andy sad?
   B: No, he *were* / *wasn't*.

3 **A:** Was it cold yesterday?
   B: No, it *wasn't* / *weren't*.

4 **A:** Were your friends at your house?
   B: Yes, *they were* / *we were*.

5 **A:** Was Anna there?
   B: Yes, *he was* / *she was*.

6 **A:** Were you late to work?
   B: No, we *wasn't* / *weren't*.

2 Complete the questions with *Was* or *Were*. Then write short answers.

1 _Were_ you at home last night?   ✔ _Yes, I was._
2 _____ Oliver happy yesterday?   ✘ _____
3 _____ you and Ted at the cinema together? ✔ _____
4 _____ all your friends at your party?   ✘ _____
5 _____ I the fastest in the race?   ✔ _____
6 _____ Katy at school last Friday?   ✔ _____

3 Write questions and short answers.

1 Carla / angry yesterday ✘

   Was Carla angry yesterday?
   No, she wasn't.

2 the muffins / in the fridge / yesterday ✔

   _____

3 the muffins / good yesterday ✔

   _____

4 the muffins / next to the eggs yesterday ✘

   _____

5 the muffins / next to the pizza yesterday ✔

   _____

Now

4 Write questions with *there*. Then write short answers.

1 lots of books / in the library
   Were there lots of books in the library?
   Yes, there were.

2 a funny film / at the cinema

   _____
   _____

3 a cat / in the park

   _____
   _____

★ 5 Write questions and true answers.

1 you / at school yesterday
   Were you at school yesterday?
   _____

2 your friend / at the shops last Sunday

   _____
   _____

3 you and your family / on holiday last week

   _____
   _____

4 your parents / at home last night

   _____
   _____

5 sunny / yesterday

   _____
   _____

🔊 12 Directions

Asking for directions
Excuse me. Where's *North Street*?
I'm looking for *a library*.
How can I get to *the Science Museum*?
Is it far?

Giving directions
It's in/on *Green Street*.
Go straight on.
Go past *the cinema*.
Turn left. / Turn right.
It's on the left. / It's on the right.

Complete the directions with the words in the box.

~~Go~~   left   on   opposite
past   straight   turn

Excuse me. Where's the hospital?

1 _Go_ straight on.
2 Then _____ right.
3 Go _____ the bank.
4 Turn _____ .
5 Go _____ on and then turn right.
6 The hospital is _____ the right.
7 It's _____ the museum.

Complete the dialogue.

A: ¹*Excuse* me. I'm ² _____ for the History Museum. Is it ³ _____ ?

B: No, it's not far. It's ⁴ _____ Brown Street. Go ⁵ _____ the bank. Then ⁶ _____ right – that's Brown Street.

A: OK.

B: Go ⁷ _____ on. The museum is ⁸ _____ the left, opposite the park.

A: Thank you.

3 Look at the map. Complete the dialogues with one word in each gap.

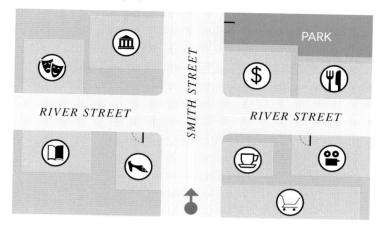

1 A: Excuse me. Where's the cinema?
   B: It's in ¹ _River_ Street. ² _____ past the supermarket. Turn ³ _____ at the ⁴ _____ . Then go straight on. The cinema is on the ⁵ _____ , opposite the ⁶ _____ .

2 A: Excuse me. How can I get to the park?
   B: It's not far. Go ⁷ _____ on. Go past the ⁸ _____ , café and the ⁹ _____ . They are all on the right. The park is next to the bank, ¹⁰ _____ the right.

3 A: Excuse me. I'm looking for the shoe shop.
   B: It's in River Street. Go ¹¹ _____ _____ . Then ¹² _____ _____ . The shoe shop is on the right.

4 Use the map in Exercise 3 to write your own dialogues.

1 A: Excuse me. Where's the library?
   B: _____
      _____

2 A: Excuse me. How can I get to the museum?
   B: _____
      _____

Extra Online Practice

Unit 5, Video and Communication
www.myenglishlab.com

An amazing city

London is a very big city today. It was very big in 1965 too. My grandpa was a boy in London then.

In 1965 London was an exciting place for fashion and music. The fashion industry was new then and there were a lot of small clothes shops. Pop music was also new, and bands like The Beatles were very popular. There were a lot of small cafés. The theatres were busy, and the museums were full of people.

Today some things about London are different. Now there are more big shops and shopping centres. There are many large cafés. The theatres have more music shows today like *Mamma Mia*. The museums are full today too. But there are more things to do today. For example, you can have a ride on the London Eye. It was new in 2000.

1 Was the London Eye in London in 1965? Read the text to find out.

2 Read the text again. Circle the correct answer.

1 London is a very (big) / *small* place.
2 In 1965 there were a lot of *big* / *small* shops in London.
3 Pop music was *old* / *new* then.
4 The museums *were* / *weren't* full in 1965.
5 Today London has got more *shopping centres* / *theatres*.
6 The London Eye is a *ride* / *museum*.

3 Read the text again and answer the questions.

1 Was the writer's grandpa a boy in 1965?
   Yes, he was.
2 Was pop music new in London in 1965?
   _____
3 Were the theatres busy in 1965?
   _____
4 Were there large cafés like Starbucks in the past? _____
5 Are there more music shows today?
   _____

4 Vocabulary **Complete the words.**

1 Let's play basketball at the s*ports* c*entre* .
2 They're making a film at the film s_____ .
3 The rides at this theme p_____ are exciting.
4 Do you want to buy some clothes at the s_____ centre?
5 You can look for your lost bag at the police s___
6 I'm going to the post o_____ to post a letter.
7 Let's buy our tickets to London at the t_____ stat
8 I like the s_____ pool, but I like the sea more!

5 Write the years.

LOOK!

| 1900 = nineteen hundred |
| 1911 = nineteen eleven |
| 2005 = two thousand and five |
| 2017 = twenty seventeen |

1 nineteen hundred   *1900*
2 nineteen fifteen   _____
3 nineteen fifty   _____
4 nineteen sixty-five   _____
5 two thousand   _____
6 twenty fifteen   _____

🔊 **13** Listen to Jimmy and his mum. Which places do they talk about? Tick (✔).

1 ✔ library

2 ☐ cinema

3 ☐ bank

4 ☐ supermarket

5 ☐ train station

6 ☐ police station

🔊 **13** Listen again. Write *yes* or *no*.

1 Is Jimmy looking at new photos? _no_

2 Was the library in Green Street? _____

3 Is there a library in Green Street now? _____

4 Was the bank next to the library? _____

5 Is there a supermarket next to the bank today?

_____

6 Is Jimmy's mum behind the train station in the next photo? _____

7 Does Jimmy think his mum's hat was nice? _____

Using adjectives

Use different adjectives to make your writing interesting.

Vocabulary Complete the adjectives.

1 There are lots of people in the village. It's very b_u s y_ . It's usually **q_ _ _t** on Sundays.

2 This **s_ _ _l** house has one bedroom, but that **b_ _** house has five.

3 I usually think museums are **i_ _ _ r_ _ _ _ _g** , but this one is **b_ _ _ _g**. There's nothing good to see.

4 The **o_ _** stadium wasn't great. But the new **m_ _ _ _n** stadium is amazing!

5 The cinema was **c_ _ _n** before the film, but after the film it was **d_ _ _y** because there was popcorn on the floor.

4 Read Joe's description of his town. Circle the adjectives that make it interesting.

My town

Hi, my name is Joe and I live in Bromley. It's a (big) town near London.

In the past my town was small and boring. There were four big shops in one street, but there wasn't a shopping centre. There was an old cinema and there were two busy burger restaurants.

Today my town is different. There's a modern shopping centre and a big cinema with a 3D screen. The new sports centre has a swimming pool and a play centre for children. Lots of people live in Bromley, so there are many interesting shops and modern cafés.

I love my town!

5 Look at two pictures of Overtown. Then complete the sentences.

In the past

Now

1 There was _____ .

2 There were _____ .

3 There wasn't _____ .

4 There weren't _____ .

5 There is _____ .

6 There are _____ .

6 Now write about Overtown. Use the adjectives in Exercise 3.

My town

Hi, my name is Alice and I live in Overtown. It's a small town.

In the past

_____

_____

Today

_____

_____

Vocabulary

1 Circle the odd one out.

0 bank shop (clean) park
1 opposite next to police station in front of
2 hospital boring restaurant theatre
3 museum hotel between film studio
4 stadium small modern quiet
5 post office supermarket busy swimming pool

◯/⑤

2 Look at the pictures. Complete the sentences with one word in each gap.

0 Let's see a film at the _cinema_ .

1 She often gets books from the _____ .

2 The coffee at this _____ is very good.

3 They often go to the _____ _____ after school.

4 Dad always meets my grandparents at the _____ _____ .

5 Grandpa sometimes takes Ken to the _____ _____ .

◯/⑤

Grammar

3 Circle the correct answer.

0 He (was)/ were sad yesterday.
1 They *was / were* at the post office, but now they're at the café.
2 I *was / were* at the hospital last week.
3 She *was / were* at the shops last Saturday.
4 We *wasn't / weren't* at the swimming pool because it was a school day.
5 Uncle Ted *wasn't / weren't* at my party.

◯/⑤

4 Complete the questions and answers.

0 A: __Were__ you at the theme park?
B: No, I wasn't.
1 A: _____ he at the film studio?
B: Yes, he was.
2 A: Were you and Greg at school at 9 a.m.?
B: Yes, we _____ .
3 A: Was Anna at the show?
B: No, she _____ .
4 A: Were you and your aunt on the same bus?
B: Yes, _____ _____ .
5 A: Were your friends here all day?
B: No, _____ _____ .

◯/⑤

Communication

5 Complete the dialogues with one word in each gap.

0 A: How can I get to the museum?
B: It's __in__ Red Street.
1 A: _____ me. Where's the toy shop?
B: It's in Green Street.
2 A: I'm looking for the supermarket.
B: Go _____ on. It's opposite the sports centre.
3 A: Where's the park?
B: _____ left. It's behind the cinema.
4 A: I'm looking for the shoe shop.
B: _____ past the theatre. It's in George Street.
5 A: Where's the school?
B: It's _____ the right.

◯/⑤

Vocabulary	◯/⑩
Grammar	◯/⑩
Communication	◯/⑤
Your total score	/ 25

Extra Online Practice

Unit 5, Language Revision
www.myenglishlab.com

Read Danny's blog about places in town.

Word blog: Towns

1 My chat room Complete the conversation.

Are you ¹b_sy, Joe? Do you want to go to the cinema?

The ²_ld one or the ³m_d_rn one?

The new one of course! There's an ⁴_nt_r_st_ng film on about robots.

Oh no! Robots are ⁵b_r_ng! Let's go to Burger Town!

No. That place is ⁶q_ _ _ t. Nobody goes there.

How about a ⁷b_g pizza?

Great idea!

2 Get more Circle the places that you connect with the words. Can you add another place?

1 tourist   *museum / library* _____

2 ticket   *park / cinema* _____

3 closed   *shop / hospital* _____

4 money   *bank / police station* _____

3 My photos Look and complete. Which place do you like best?

Maria

1 Hyde P _ _ k in London

Bob

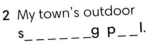

2 My town's outdoor s_ _ _ _ _ _g p_ _l.

Trisha

3 Our busy s_ _ _ _ _ _g c_ _ _ _e

Joe

4 The police s_ _ _ _ _r My dad works there!

Get more words

Oh no! We're in a traffic jam.

Fun Spot

Find and circle the things which are different. In your notebook, write six differences.

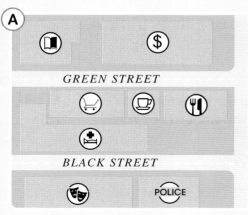

A

GREEN STREET

RED STREET

PARK

BLACK STREET

POLICE

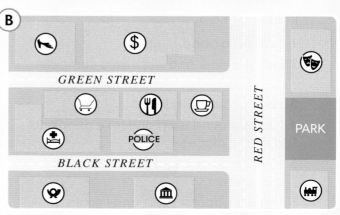

B

GREEN STREET

RED STREET

PARK

POLICE

BLACK STREET

In Picture A, there is a library in Green Street.

6 Just the job

6.1 Vocabulary

1 Circle the correct word.

1 teacher / (doctor)

2 farmer / builder

3 chef / vet

4 police officer / office worker

5 footballer / shop assistant

6 bus driver / pilot

2 Can you name the jobs? Use the verbs in blue for help.

1 I sing in a band. _singer_

2 I sit at a desk and work on a computer. _____

3 I build houses and flats. _____

4 I drive around town and take people to different places. _____

5 I fly planes and take people to other countries. _____

6 I play a popular sport and I score goals. _____

3 Complete the text with names of jobs.

Hi, I'm Mark and this is my family. You can see me with my dad on the left. Dad loves cooking but he isn't a ¹_chef_ . He works at the hospital, but he isn't a doctor. He's a ²_____ . Mum works at my sister's school. She's a French ³_____ . My grandpa and grandma work too. Grandma is a great ⁴_____ and she paints beautiful pictures. She sells them in a shop. Grandpa works in her shop – he's her ⁵_____ . I like animals and when I grow up I want to be a ⁶_____ so I can look after people's pets.

4 Complete the dialogue with the words in the box.

| be   grow   hospital   people   police station |
| restaurant   school |

Chris: What do you want to ¹_____be_____ when you ²_____ up?

Kelly: I think I want to be a teacher at a ³_____ in my town. But I also like cooking, so I sometimes think I want to work in a ⁴_____ and be a chef. What about you?

Chris: My dad wants me to be a police officer like h and work at the ⁵_____ . It's a good idea because I like helping ⁶_____ . But I'd like study to be a doctor and work at the ⁷_____

5 Complete the table for you. What do you want to be? Why?

jobs I like: _____ , _____

jobs I don't like: _____ , _____

jobs I like a lot: _____ , _____

I want to be _____ because _____ .

> I remember that!

Past Simple affirmative: regular verbs

+
I **played** football.
You **played** football.
He/She/It **played** football.
We/You/They **played** football.

LOOK!
cook – cooked
arrive – arrived
tidy – tidied
stop – stopped

Complete the table with the Past Simple forms of verbs in the box.

~~cook~~ cry cycle jump hop like
phone plan stay stop study try

-ed	-ied	-d	double letter + -ed
cooked	____	____	____
____	____	____	____
____	____	____	____

Choose a verb and complete the sentences with the Past Simple forms.

1 My aunt *phoned* me last Saturday on my mobile. (phone)/ talk

2 She _____ me to Harry's birthday party. *invite / arrive*

3 I _____ on the way at the toy shop for a present. *play / stop*

4 Harry and his friends _____ to music. *dance / like*

5 I _____ my aunt with the food. *cook / help*

6 Harry _____ his party! *look / like*

LOOK! Her babysitter was ill two days ago.

3 Look and write time expressions with *ago*.

Now it is: `04:00` | May | Tuesday

1 `03:00` *an hour ago*

2 `03:50` _____

3 March _____

4 Saturday _____

✱ **4 Read the information. Than make sentences using the Past Simple affirmative and *ago*.**

1 Tom's last football game was Friday last week. Today is Friday again.
   Tom played football a week ago.

2 Your text was on my phone at 9.15. It's now 9.20.
   You _____ .

3 It's August. Our visit to London was last August.
   We _____ .

4 Her room was tidy at 9 o'clock. It's now 10 o'clock.
   She _____ .

5 Complete the table with your own ideas.

1 A friend you texted	Name: _____ When: _____
2 A family member a meal he/she cooked	Name: _____ Meal: _____ When: _____
3 A family member you visited	Name: _____ When: _____
4 Two or more friends you played sport with	Sport: _____ When: _____ Where: _____

✱ **6 Make sentences using your ideas in the table. Use the Past Simple affirmative and *ago* or *last*.**

1 I _____ .

2 My _____ .

3 I _____ .

4 My friends and I _____ .

Extra Online Practice

Unit 6, Video and Grammar
www.myenglishlab.com

6.3 Grammar

1 Complete the crossword with the Past Simple affirmative of the verbs.

Across

- 2 have
- 3 go
- 5 drink
- 7 come

Down

- 1 make
- 4 take
- 6 eat
- 8 meet

Crossword: 1 M / A / D / E, 2 _A_, 3 _E_, 4, 5, 6, 7, 8

2 Write the verbs in the Past Simple affirmative.

1 We ___had___ (have) lunch at 2 o'clock yesterday.

2 I _____ (make) a pizza last Sunday.

3 We _____ (go) to the cinema last month.

4 You _____ (take) a photo of me two minutes ago.

5 They _____ (drink) tea after the meal yesterday evening.

6 I _____ (eat) a sandwich for lunch an hour ago.

7 We first _____ (meet) three years ago.

8 Everyone _____ (come) to my party last Saturday.

3 Big Al is thinking about the past. Complete the sentences with the verbs from Exercise 1 in the Past Simple affirmative.

Last week

1 Pete _made_ a big pizza.

2 Rocco and I _____ to the cinema.

3 Carla _____ a selfie in the park.

4 We _____ a lot of fun at a party.

5 I _____ Rocco outside a café.

6 Carla _____ to my house for dinner.

4 Complete the sentences. Use the verbs in the Past Simple affirmative and the words in the box.

> a hot dog   a lemon cake   crisps   tea
> the sea   your house

1 I usually have a sandwich for lunch, but yesterday I _had a hot dog_ .

2 We sometimes eat popcorn at the cinema, but last Friday we _____ .

3 Mum often makes a chocolate cake, but last week she _____ .

4 My grandparents usually drink coffee, but yesterday they _____ .

5 Tim usually takes photos of people, but last holiday he _____ .

6 You often come to my house, but last Monday I _____ .

✸ 5 Write sentences that are true for you. Use the verbs in brackets in the Past Simple affirmative.

1 I (have) _____ for dinner yesterday.
I had chicken and chips for dinner yesterday.

2 I first (meet) my best friend _____ ago.

_____

3 I (go) on holiday last _____ .

_____

4 I (eat) pizza _____ ago.

_____

14 Asking for and giving permission

Can I borrow *a pen*, please?
Yes, you can. / No, sorry, you can't. /
Sure, no problem.
Is it OK if I *use your mobile*?
No, sorry, it isn't OK. / Oh, all right. /
Yes, that's fine.

Complete the questions and answers.

1 **A:** Is it OK ___if___ I use your ___mobile___ ?

   B: _____ , all right.

2 **A:** _____ I borrow your _____ , please?

   B: Sure, no _____ .

3 **A:** Is it _____ if I use your _____ ?

   B: Yes, that's _____ .

4 **A:** Can I _____ your _____ , please?

   B: _____ , you can.

5 **A:** Can I borrow your _____ , _____ ?

   B: No, _____ , you can't.

LOOK!

Please can I go to the party?
Can I go to the party, **please**?

Write two questions asking for permission with *please* for each situation.

1 You want to go to the cinema.
   a *Please can I go to the cinema?*
   b *Can I go to the cinema, please?*

2 You want to use your dad's laptop.
   a _____
   b _____

3 You want to borrow a friend's mobile.
   a _____
   b _____

3 Complete the dialogues. Sometimes there is more than one answer.

> Can I borrow your mobile, please?   No, it isn't.
> ~~Is it OK if I use yours?~~   Please can I go to the cinema?   Sure, no problem.   Yes, you can.

Dialogue 1

Elena: We've got a Maths test today. Have you got your calculator this time?

Tom: Oh no, I forgot it. ¹*Is it OK if I use yours?*

Elena: ² _____ I need it for the test!

Tom: OK, I understand. I hope the test is easy!

Dialogue 2

Jess: Hi Tom. Do you want to go to the cinema?

Matt: Sure, but I have to ask my mum first. ³ _____ I don't have my phone with me.

Jess: ⁴ _____ Here you are.

Matt: Thanks. Oh, hi mum. ⁵ _____

Mum: ⁶ _____

4 Look at the notes and write a dialogue asking for permission.

> Who: Paul and Leo
> Where: go to the swimming pool
> Ask Leo's dad for permission
> Permission: No
> Why: homework

Paul: _____

Leo: _____
_____

Dad: _____

Leo: _____

5 In your notebook, write a dialogue asking for permission. Use these notes.

> Who: Anna and Milly
> Where: go shopping
> Ask Milly's grandma for permission
> Permission: Yes

Extra Online Practice

Unit 6, Video and Communication
www.myenglishlab.com

Do you think that a child's life was different in the past? I asked my dad and grandpa.

Dad

When I was a boy I helped my mum with jobs in the house every weekend. She gave me 50p when I washed the car or I tidied the living room. It wasn't a lot of money, but I did many jobs! When I had the money, I bought an expensive football. It was really cool and all my friends liked it.

Grandpa

My family was poor, so there wasn't any pocket money! But I wanted some money, so I got a Saturday job at a restaurant. I washed the dishes and the floor, and I put the plates on the tables. I made a lot of money and when I was sixteen I bought a bicycle. I went everywhere on that bike!

1 Read the article and choose the best title. Circle the correct answer.

  a The house jobs my dad did

  b How Grandpa bought a bike

  c When Dad and Grandpa were children

2 Read the text again. Write D (Dad), G (Grandpa) or B (both).

  1 He helped his mum in the house.   _D_

  2 His family was poor.   ____

  3 He washed something for money.   ____

  4 He worked at a restaurant.   ____

  5 He bought a football.   ____

  6 He bought a bicycle.   ____

3 Read the text again. Circle T (true) or F (false).

  1 Dad helped his mum every Saturday and Sunday.   (T)/ F

  2 Dad's mum gave him a lot of money.   T / F

  3 Dad tidied the living room.   T / F

  4 Dad's friends liked his football.   T / F

  5 Grandpa worked every Sunday.   T / F

  6 Grandpa bought a bike when he was 15.   T / F

4 **Vocabulary** Match the sentence halves.

  Yesterday …

  1 [b] Rob washed the   **a** his room.

  2 [ ] He tidied   **b** car.

  3 [ ] He emptied   **c** the dog.

  4 [ ] He walked   **d** his bed.

  5 [ ] He did   **e** the dishes.

  6 [ ] He made   **f** the shopping.

  7 [ ] He washed   **g** his sister.

  8 [ ] He looked after   **h** the bin.

5 Name the jobs these children did at home in the pas

1 He _____ .

2 She _____ .

3 They _____

🔊 15 **What did Nick do last Saturday? Listen and circle the correct answer.**

1 Nick's (uncle)/ *grandfather* visited.
2 They played *basketball / football*.
3 They had lunch at *a restaurant / home*.
4 They went to the *theatre / cinema*.

🔊 15 **Listen again. Complete the sentences with one word in each gap.**

1 Nick had a fun day last _Saturday_ .
2 First, Nick went to the _____ .
3 He scored _____ goals.
4 Nick ate _____ cheeseburgers.
5 Nick and Ted drank _____ .
6 The _____ was really exciting.
7 Gary and Ted went home at _____ o'clock.

First, Then, After that

First, we visited Madame Tussaud's.
Then, we went to the London Aquarium.
After that, we went to a Mexican restaurant.

Complete Elena's blog. Use the verbs in brackets in the Past Simple affirmative.

A day out at the beach
by Elena

☐ First, we ¹*went* (go) to the beach and we went swimming. But the sea ²_____ (be) cold, so we ³_____ (get) out quickly!

☐ After that, we ⁴_____ (have) a picnic on the sand. We ⁵_____ (eat) sandwiches and ⁶_____ (drink) coke. Mum came and took us home in her car. We arrived home at 4 o'clock. It was a great day out!

☐ Then we ⁷_____ (play) beach volleyball. Amy and I ⁸_____ (be) Team A and the boys were Team B. It was a lot of fun. Amy and I were the winners!

☐ 1 Last Sunday I went to the beach with my friends.

Number the paragraphs above in the right order 1–4.

5 **Circle the things you like for a great day out.**

beach
restaurant
cinema
stadium
park

hot dogs
sandwiches
popcorn
milkshakes
lemonade
water

photos
film
sports
bus
train
car

6 **Write about a day out. You can use your ideas from Exercise 5 and your own ideas. Remember to use *First*, *Then* and *After that*.**

_____ by _____
Last _____ *I* _____
_____
_____
_____
_____
_____
_____
_____
We arrived home at _____
_____
It was _____
_____
_____

Check yourself!

Vocabulary

1 Circle the correct word.

0 My aunt is a (teacher)/ pilot at my school.

1 Fred went to the hospital to see a *doctor* / *vet* after hitting his head.

2 The *nurse* / *farmer* gives food to the animals every morning.

3 The *chef* / *artist* at this restaurant cooks delicious meals.

4 Tina is an *office worker* / *a shop assistant* and she sells shoes.

5 Craig is a *bus driver* / *singer* so he knows all the places in town.

☐/⑤

2 Look at the pictures. Complete the sentences with one word in each gap.

0 Please __tidy__ your room.

1 I _____ the _____ every night.

2 They _____ the _____ three times a day.

3 We _____ the _____ at the weekend.

4 I often _____ _____ my sister .

5 We _____ the _____ at the supermarket.

☐/⑤

Grammar

3 Complete the sentences with verbs in the box. Use the Past Simple affirmative.

> clean   cycle   play   stop   study   ~~text~~

0 Sandra __texted__ her friend on her mobile a minute ago.

1 We _____ all evening yesterday for the test.

2 He _____ to work last Monday on his bike.

3 I _____ the car at the red light one minute ago.

4 The friends _____ basketball at the sports centre yesterday.

5 They _____ the house after the party, so today it looks great.

☐/⑤

4 Complete the sentences with the Past Simple affirmative of the correct verb.

0 (have)/ do

I __had__ lunch at 2 p.m. yesterday.

1 *go / meet*

I _____ Ted at the cinema an hour a

2 *eat / drink*

Yesterday Mum _____ tea after din

3 *make / buy*

We _____ some cakes at the supermarket.

4 *take / put*

Jim _____ lots of photos on holiday last year.

5 *give / do*

Dad _____ me a watch for my last birthday.

☐

Communication

5 Complete the dialogue with one word i each gap.

Pam: Please ⁰__can__ I borrow your laptop, dad?

Dad: No, ¹_____ , you can't. I'm using Why do you need it?

Pam: I'm planning a project for school c I want to look at the Internet.

Dad: Is it OK ²_____ I look at your not

Pam: Yes, that's ³_____ . Here.

Dad: They're good.

Pam: Come on, dad. Can I use your laptop, ⁴_____ ? Just for an hou

Dad: Oh, ⁵_____ _____ .

☐

Vocabulary	☐	/⑴
Grammar	☐	/⑴
Communication	☐	/☐
Your total score		/ 2

Extra Online Practice

Unit 6, Language Revision
www.myenglishlab.com

Word blog: Jobs

1 My photos Complete the sentences.

1 This is my dad and my uncle. They're _____ _____ .

2 Here's my mum. She's a _____ at a big farm.

3 Grandma works in a flower shop. She's a _____ _____ .

4 Grandpa was a _____ . He doesn't work now, but he likes fixing the house.

2 My forum Complete the words.

Maria
1 I love painting flowers, so I want to be an a _ _ _ _ t . But I also want to be a n _ _ _ e because I like looking after people. Or a d _ _ _ _ r .

Bob
2 I'm not sure. I like driving so maybe I want to be a b _ _ d _ _ _ _ r ! Or perhaps a p _ _ _ t , because I like flying! I don't want to be an o _ _ _ _ e w _ _ _ _ r because I don't like being indoors all day.

Trisha
3 I want to live on a farm and be a f _ _ _ _ r ! Or a Science t _ _ _ _ _ r in a school. Or a f _ _ _ _ _ _ _ _ r because I love sport! I don't know!

Joe
4 I love cooking so I want to be a c _ _ f ! Or a s _ _ _ _ r , because I am good at singing!

3 Get more Sometimes we can say something in different ways. Do you know the different verbs that fit these sentences?

1 Let's have a pizza. = Let's e *a t* a pizza.

2 I'd like to a have cup of coffee. = I'd like to d _ _ _ _ a cup of coffee.

3 Can you do the dishes, please? = Can you w _ _ _ the dishes, please?

4 What job do you do? = What job do you h _ _ _ ?

5 Let's get some fruit from the shops. = Let's b _ _ some fruit from the shops.

Get more words

You got the job. Congratulations!

Strange things happened yesterday! Write five sentences about the picture.

Fun Spot

An artist emptied the bin.

_____

_____

_____

_____

My cool places

My number one cool place this week is a city. It's Liverpool! People often think Liverpool is very busy and dirty. Well, it's busy but it's cleaner than you think. It's also very interesting and you can do some interesting things.

I went there with my family last weekend to visit my Uncle Robert. He's a police officer so he knows the city very well. He took us to China Town for dinner on Friday evening. On Saturday morning we went to the Museum of Liverpool. It's modern and very cool. Here's an interesting fact. Only London has more museums than Liverpool. Saturday afternoon was even better. We saw a football game at Liverpool FC's stadium, Anfield Road. Wow!

Before we came home on Sunday, I went for a long walk with dad and my uncle … on the beach! Mum and my sister didn't come. They went shopping in Liverpool One, a very big shopping centre. Liverpool is awesome.

John

Reading and Writing

1 **Read the text. Circle T (true) or F (false).**

0 Some people think Liverpool is busy
  and dirty. (T)/ F
1 John visited Liverpool a month ago. T / F
2 John's Uncle Robert is a police officer. T / F
3 Uncle Robert didn't go to China Town. T / F
4 John liked the Museum of Liverpool. T / F
5 They went to a football game on Sunday. T / F
6 There are a lot of shops in Liverpool One. T / F

☐/⑥

2 **Complete the text with the words in the box. There are three extra words.**

> bag   drank   happy   met   post office   ran
> surprised   ~~swimming pool~~   waiter

I love swimming! Last Saturday morning I had a swimming lesson at my town's ⁰ *swimming pool*. After the lesson, I looked at my mobile phone. There was a text message from my friend Marisa: 'Come to Ice Cream Café!'

I don't know the town centre very well because I'm new here. 'It's in the High Street', a friendly girl at the swimming pool said. 'Go past the ¹ _____ and turn left. It's on the right next to the bank.' When I arrived at the café I was ² _____ because Marisa wasn't there. There was just one ³ _____ in the café and there wasn't any mus. It was very boring. I wanted to phone Marisa but m phone wasn't in my ⁴_____ ! What a mess! I ⁵_____ back to the swimming pool. Yes! My phone was there. I phoned Marisa. 'I know wha happened!' she said. 'Guess what? There are two I Cream Cafés in the centre!'

☐/(

3 **Now choose the best name for the story. Tick (✔ one box.**

☐ Last Saturday morning
☐ The swimming pool
☐ A boring café

☐/(

4 **Jane had fun with her friends last Saturday. Write sentences about her day.**

0 we / take / a lot of selfies / in the morning
  We took a lot of selfies in the morning.

1 my photos / be / fantastic

_____

2 mum / make / a yummy pizza / for lunch

_____

3 dad / give me / my pocket money

_____

4 we / go / cinema / in the afternoon

_____

5 we / watch the film / and / eat ice cream

_____

☐/(

Listening

🔊 16 Rob is showing his mum some photos of a school trip on his school website. Listen and match names 0–4 to pictures A–F. There is one extra picture.

0 [c] John   3 [ ] Jerry

1 [ ] Mandy   4 [ ] Rob

2 [ ] Gemma

A

B

C

D

E

F

◯/④

Communication

6 Look at the pictures of the White family on a day out. Match pictures 0–4 to sentences a–g. There are two extra sentences.

a There it is!

b He's a pilot.

c Can I borrow some money?

d Go past the theatre and turn right.

e Let's have a drink first.

f Oh, all right!

g Excuse me. Where's the Science Museum?

◯/④

Reading and Writing ◯/⑰

Listening ◯/④

Communication ◯/④

Your total score   / 25

Going places

7.1 Vocabulary

1 Label the pictures with these words.

| bus car motorbike plane taxi ~~train~~ |

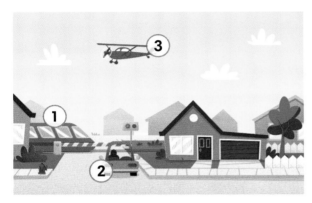

1 _train_   2 _____   3 _____

4 _____   5 _____   6 _____

2 Read the definitions and name the transport.

1 This is very long and it has lots of wheels. It runs on streets. _tram_

2 You can go to an island on this over water. _____

3 This flies in the air. _____

4 This has four wheels. Many families have got one. _____

5 Children have got these and they can ride them in the park. _____

LOOK!

I go to school by car / by train / by boat.
I go to school on foot. = I walk to school.

3 Read and circle the correct answer.

This is Emily and she's 12. She lives on a farm. It's a long way from her school. There isn't a ¹_tram_ / _bike_ near her house and she doesn't go ²_by_ / _on_ train because it's expensive. It's too far to go ³_by_ / _on_ foot, so Emily usually rides her ⁴_motorbike_ / _bike_ to school. It takes her 30 minutes! When it rains her mum drives her to school in her ⁵_boat_ / _car_.

4 Complete the text with the words in the box.

| ~~arrived~~   got off   got on   left   took |

Last weekend I went to London by train. I ¹_arrived_ at 10 o'clock. Then, I ²_____ the underground to the Science museum. After that, I ³_____ a red bus and sat at the top. I ⁴_____ at the station. I ran for the train because I only had five minutes before it ⁵_____ !

5 Complete the sentences with one word in each gap

1 I don't like _planes_ because I'm scared of flying.

2 He goes to school _____ foot.

3 The train _____ in five minutes so let's run to the station.

4 Mum goes to work _____ tram.

5 Please let the people get off the bus first before you get _____ and sit down.

6 This part of the road is only for _____ , so cyclists are safe.

6 Complete the sentences for you.

I remem
that!

1 I usually go to school _____ .

2 I never go to school _____ .

3 My family sometimes goes to the shops _____

4 We often travel on holiday _____ .

Past Simple negative

Regular verbs

I/You/He/She/It/We/They
didn't stay at home.

Irregular verbs

I/You/He/She/It/We/They
didn't sleep well.

didn't = did not

1 Complete the table.

	+	−
go	went	¹ *didn't go*
sleep	slept	² _____
take	³ _____	didn't take
have	⁴ _____	didn't have
eat	ate	⁵ _____
drink	drank	⁶ _____
bring	⁷ _____	didn't bring
meet	⁸ _____	didn't meet

2 Write the opposite.

1 Elena and Amy stayed at home.
Elena and Amy *didn't stay* at home.

2 The first night Elena slept well.
The first night Elena _____ well.

3 The spider went inside Elena's sleeping bag.
The spider _____ inside Elena's sleeping bag.

4 Elena brought her coat.
Elena _____ her coat.

5 That evening they ate at a restaurant.
That evening they _____ at a restaurant.

3 Look at the pictures and complete the sentences.

1 **eat**
Tim _ate_ pizza at the pizzeria.
He _didn't eat_ ice cream.

2 **drink**
Dad _____ water.
He _____ coffee.

3 **wear**
Tina _____ a hat.
She _____ a coat.

4 **go**
Mum and Stan _____ to the supermarket.
They _____ to the toy shop.

4 **Vocabulary** What can you see in the picture? Tick (✔).

- ☐ backpack
- ☐ camera
- ☐ guidebook
- ☐ sleeping bag
- ☐ suitcase
- ☐ sunglasses
- ☐ tent
- ☐ torch

✳ 5 Circle true (T) or false (F) for you. Correct the false sentences.

1 I went to school last Saturday. T / F
_____

2 My friend texted me an hour ago. T / F
_____

3 We stayed in a tent on our last holiday. T / F
_____

4 I took a plane last summer. T / F
_____

5 I brought my sunglasses to school on Monday. T / F
_____

Extra Online Practice

Unit 7, Video and Grammar
www.myenglishlab.com

Grammar

Past Simple questions and short answers

?	Short answers
Did I/you **have** a good time?	Yes, I **did**. / No, I **didn't**.
Did he/she/it **have** a good time?	Yes, he/she/it **did**. / No, he/she/it **didn't**.
Did we/you/they **have** a good time?	Yes, we/you/they **did**. No, we/you/they **didn't**.
Where **did** you **go**? What **did** you **do**?	I went to Rome. I ate spaghetti.

1 Circle the correct answer.

Big Al: Hi Rocco. Did you ¹(have)/ had fun yesterday?

Rocco: Yes, I ²did / didn't. I went to the park with Carla.

Big Al: Did you ³played / play football?

Rocco: No, we ⁴did / didn't. We had a picnic.

Big Al: ⁵What did / Did you eat?

Rocco: We ate sandwiches, apples and bananas.

Big Al: ⁶What did / Did you drink lemonade?

Rocco: No. We got a milkshake at the park café.

2 Put the words in the correct order to make questions. Then answer them. Use short answers.

 **A**  **B**

A 1 go they Did last on holiday weekend ?

  Did they go on holiday last weekend?

  ✔ _Yes, they did._

  2 sleep Did a tent the boy in ?

  _____

  ✗ _____

B 3 yesterday grandparents shopping Did your go ?

  _____

  ✔ _____

  4 buy your Did a camera granny new ?

  _____

  ✗ _____

3 Complete the questions with one word in each gap.

1 A: _What_ did you buy?

  B: I bought a T-shirt.

2 A: _____ did you get it?

  B: I got it at the museum.

3 A: _____ did you go to the museum?

  B: I went last Saturday.

4 A: _____ did you get there?

  B: I took the underground.

5 A: _____ did you take the underground?

  B: Because it's the fastest.

4 Vocabulary Match 1–7 to a–g.

1 [c] go   a a souvenir
2 [ ] visit   b photos
3 [ ] make   c sightseeing
4 [ ] eat   d friends
5 [ ] stay   e a museum
6 [ ] take   f at a restaurant
7 [ ] buy   g in a hotel

✱ 5 Look at the pictures. Write questions and short answers.

Fred's last holiday in France

1 _Did Fred take a lot of photos?_

  Yes, _____ .

2 _____

  _____

3 _____

  _____

4 _____

  _____

🔊 17 Buying a ticket

A: I'd like a ticket to *London*, please.
B: Here you are.
A: How much is it?
B: It's *ten pounds twenty*, please.
A: What time does the train leave?
B: At *seven thirty*.
A: What time does it arrive?
B: At *eight*.
A: Thanks.

1 Complete the dialogue with sentences a–e. There is one extra sentence.

Boy: I'd like two tickets to York, please.
Woman: ¹*Here you are.*
Boy: How much is it?
Woman: ² _____
Boy: What time does the train leave?
Woman: ³ _____
Boy: What time does it arrive?
Woman: ⁴ _____

a At 10 a.m.
b It's ten pounds, please.
c Here you are.
d They're ten.
e At 10.30 a.m.

LOOK!

Prices
£10.50 = ten pounds fifty
£7.25 = seven pounds twenty-five
£0.50 = fifty pence

2 Match 1–5 to a–e.

1 [b] £2.50   **a** thirty pounds forty
2 [ ] £0.75   **b** two pounds fifty
3 [ ] £30.40   **c** seventy-five pence
4 [ ] £22.60   **d** thirty pence
5 [ ] £0.30   **e** twenty-two pounds sixty

3 Read the dialogue and complete the ticket.

> **Train Ticket** 🚄
> From: *London*   To: [____]
> Price: £ [____]
> Leave: [ ]:[ ]   Arrive: [ ]:[ ]

A: What time does the next train from London to Oxford leave?
B: At quarter past one.
A: I'd like one ticket, please.
B: Here you are.
A: How much is it?
B: It's twelve pounds fifty, please.
A: What time does it arrive in Oxford?
B: At half past three.

4 Complete the ticket with your own ideas.

> **Train Ticket** 🚄
> From: [____]   To: [____]
> Price: £ [____]
> Leave: [ ]:[ ]   Arrive: [ ]:[ ]

5 Use your ideas from Exercise 4 to write a dialogue about buying a ticket.

You: _____
Man: _____
You: _____
Man: _____
You: _____
Man: _____

Extra Online Practice

 Unit 7, Video and Communication
www.myenglishlab.com

7.5 Reading

In 1953, the explorer Edmund Hillary travelled to the Himalayan Mountains with two climbing teams. He was on an expedition to climb the tallest mountain in the world – Mount Everest. The mountain was very dangerous. There was snow and ice, and it was very cold. There were two teams for the climb to the top. The first team tried, but they didn't get there.

Edmund Hillary and his guide Tenzing Norgay were the second team. They started to climb the mountain. Their backpacks were heavy – 14 kg! They had a tent, food and a camera with them. On 29th May, Edmund Hillary and Tenzing Norgay arrived at the top of Mount Everest. Edmund got there first. Edmund took photos of Tenzing and the tall mountain, but he didn't want Tenzing to take a photo of him. So there isn't a photo of Edmund Hillary on the top of the world!

1 Read the text quickly. Answer the question.

How many people got to the top of Mount Everest on May 29th? _____

2 Read the text again. Circle T (true), F (false) or NI (no information).

1 The expedition was in the Himalayan Mountains. (T)/ F / NI
2 The weather wasn't cold. T / F / NI
3 There were three men on the first team. T / F / NI
4 The first team didn't get to the top. T / F / NI
5 Edmund Hillary got to the top before Tenzing Norgay. T / F / NI
6 They were very tired. T / F / NI
7 Tenzing didn't want Edmund to take his photo. T / F / NI
8 There isn't a photo of Edmund on the top of Mount Everest. T / F / NI

3 Read the text again. Answer the questions.

1 When did this expedition happen? _1953_
2 What was the name of the mountain? _____
3 How many teams were there? _____
4 How heavy were the backpacks? _____
5 Who arrived at the top first? _____
6 Why isn't there a photo of Edmund at the top? _____

4 Look at the highlighted words in the text. Put them in the correct place in the table.

Nouns	Adjectives	Verbs
explorer	_____	_____
_____	_____	_____
_____	_____	_____
_____	_____	_____

1 Label the pictures.

1 c_amera_ 2 m_____ 3 t_____
p_____

4 g_____ 5 s_____ 6 t_____

18 Listen to Dave and Penny. What do they talk about? Tick (✔) the pictures in Exercise 1.

18 Listen again. Circle the correct answer.

1 Where did Penny stay?

 a    ⓑ

2 What did she do every day?

 a    b

3 What did she take the photos with?

 a   b

4 What did she download her photos to?

 a   b

5 What was the weather like?

 a    b

A postcard

We're having a lovely time in …
Lots of love,   There are lots of …
Yesterday we went to …   Dear …,
See you soon!   Hi …!   We're staying in …

4 Complete the postcard with phrases in the box above.

1 _Hi_ Josh!
2 _____ London.
It's cloudy here, but it isn't cold.
We're staying in a nice hotel.
(A) 3 _____ museums and cafés, but the hotel isn't near the big shops.
(B) 4 _____ the Science Museum and I bought some souvenirs. For dinner we had cheeseburgers and chips and it was great!
(C) Today we are at the river. There's a boat here that goes to Tower Bridge. It leaves in 20 minutes! I hope it's fun!
5 _____ Terry

5 Match topics (1–6) to the paragraphs in Josh's postcard. Write A, B or C.

1 [B] food   4 [ ] town
2 [ ] weather   5 [ ] transport
3 [ ] place to stay 6 [ ] place to visit

6 Write a postcard to a friend. Use the questions to help you.

1 Where are you?
2 Where are you staying?
3 What's the weather like?
4 What did you do/eat/drink yesterday?
5 What are you doing today?

Check yourself!

Vocabulary

1 Complete the word groups with the words in the box.

> backpack   hotel   sightseeing
> sleeping bag   taxi   ~~train~~

0 tram, underground, _train_
1 suitcase, bag, _____
2 car, bus, _____
3 campsite, hostel, _____
4 souvenir, museum, _____
5 torch, tent, _____

◻/⑤

2 Look at the pictures. Complete the sentences with one word in each gap.

0 Be careful when you get _on_ the _boat_ .

1 I go to school _____ _____ .

2 Dad always _____ lots of _____ of us on holiday.

3 Terry always goes to work _____ _____ .

4 Let's _____ at this burger _____ .

5 Grandma gets _____ the _____ at this stop.

◻/⑤

Grammar

3 Complete the sentences.

0 Vicky watched TV. She _didn't watch_ a DVD.
1 Mum and Dad went to a café. They _____ to a restaurant.
2 I took a bus to school. I _____ a taxi.
3 Mary wore a dress. She _____ jeans.
4 Paul studied for a Maths test. He _____ for a Geography test.
5 The bus stopped outside the bank. But it _____ outside the museum.

◻/(

4 Complete questions 1–2 and short answers 3–5.

0 A: _Did you stay_ (you / stay) in a hotel in London
  B: Yes, I did.
1 A: _____ (he / leave) at 9 a.m.?
  B: Yes, he did.
2 A: _____ (your dad / cook) dinner last n
  B: No, he didn't.
3 A: Did your mum have coffee for breakfast?
  B: ✔ _____
4 A: Did he go to school yesterday?
  B: ✔ _____
5 A: Did they arrive at 3 p.m.?
  B: ✗ _____

◻/(

Communication

5 Complete the dialogue with one word in each gap

A: I'd ⁰_like_ a ticket to Manchester, ¹_____ .
B: ²_____ you are.
A: ³_____ much is it?
B: It's twenty pounds forty, please.
A: What time ⁴_____ the train leave?
B: At ten fifteen.
A: What time does it ⁵_____ ?
B: Two hours later. At twelve fifteen.

◻/(

Vocabulary ◻/(10
Grammar ◻/(10
Communication ◻/(5
Your total score ___ / 25

Extra Online Practice

Unit 7, Language Revision
www.myenglishlab.com

Read Joe's blog about his holiday.

Word blog: Travel

1 My photos Complete the sentences.

Check out my photos from my amazing holiday in Greece!

1 I went s_____ every day. I even saw the Parthenon!

2 I took a big b_____ to an island called Santorini.

3 I v_____ the Archaeological M_____ .

4 I s_____ in a beautiful h_____ on the island.

2 My chat room Complete the conversation.

I know you're scared of flying, so did you go by ¹pl_ _e?

No, I didn't. I took the ²t_ai_! And then my uncle drove me in his ³t_ _i! I also got the ⁴b_s and the ⁵t_ _m in Athens. Oh, and the ⁶und_ _gr_ _ _d is super fast!

What else did you do in Athens?

I bought lots of ⁷s_ _v_ _irs! My ⁸s_ _tc_se was full! I took lots of ⁹p_ _ _os with my new ¹⁰c_m_ _a. And I ¹¹a_e at lots of Greek ¹²r_ _t_ _r_nts.

3 Get more Underline the phrases with the verb *go*.

Last year we didn't know where to go on holiday. But then my dad said: 'Let's travel around Europe' I wanted to go on a journey by train and my sister wanted to go camping. 'OK' said my dad. Mum wanted to go to London first and to go sightseeing, so that's where we started. Then we got the train to Paris. Three weeks later, we went home! We were happy, but tired!

Get more words

Have a good trip!

What did they do? Tick (✔) the sentences that match the picture.

Fun Spot

1 ☐ We stayed at a hotel.
2 ☐ We stayed at a campsite.
3 ☐ Mum read a lot of magazines.
4 ☐ Dad slept in his sleeping bag.
5 ☐ We did some sightseeing.
6 ☐ I swam in the sea.
7 ☐ I rode my bike.
8 ☐ My dog made friends.

1 Complete the sentences with the words in the box.

~~barbecue~~   birthday party
dance show   sleepover

1 Dad's cooking meat on the _barbecue_ .

2 We're having a _____ at Tracy's house tonight!

3 We're enjoying a great _____ ! I'm 12 today!

4 Maria is doing ballet in the _____ .

2 Complete the events.

Hi, I'm Anna. The people in my family do interesting things. My grandad loves sport so he usually sees a football [1] _m a t c h_ at the weekend at the stadium. Mum likes the theatre so she often sees a [2] _ _ _ _ . I like wearing costumes so I always have a fancy [3] _ _ _ _ _ party on my birthday. My older brother James is a good singer. He loves music and often goes to a [4] _ _ _ _ _ _ _ to hear his favourite band. My uncle, Paul, is also a good singer. He wants to be famous, so he is in a [5] _ _ _ _ _ _ competition at the moment. I hope he wins! Dad loves being outdoors. So he often takes us to the park for a [6] _ _ _ _ _ _ . He makes all the sandwiches!

3 Match 1–6 to a–f.

1 [b] the seventh   **a** 24th
2 [ ] the first   **b** 7th
3 [ ] the thirtieth   **c** 2nd
4 [ ] the twenty-fourth   **d** 1st
5 [ ] the thirteenth   **e** 13th
6 [ ] the second   **f** 30th

LOOK! Dates
1st May = the first of May
23rd June = the twenty-third of June

4 Look at the diary. Answer the questions.

APRIL
Mon 23 History test
Tue 24 school play
Wedn 25
Thu 26 holiday for everyone!
Fri 27 Mark's birthday party
Sat 28 school football competition

1 When is Mark's birthday?
on the twenty-seventh of April
2 When does everyone have a holiday?
_____
3 When is the school play?
_____
4 When is the school football competition?
_____
5 When is the History test?
_____
_____

I remember that!

5 Write an event for each definition. Tick (✔) the ones you do.

1 You watch this at a theatre. [ ] _play_
2 You spend a night at a friend's house. [ ] _____
3 You wear a costume to this party. [ ] _____
4 You cook a meal outdoors with sausages for this. [ ] _____

be going to

+	−
I'm going to play.	I'm not going to play.
You're going to play.	You aren't going to play.
He/She/It's going to play.	He/She/It isn't going to play.
We/You/They're going to play.	We/You/They aren't going to play.

be going to

?	Short answers
Am I going to play?	Yes, I am. / No, I'm not.
Are you going to play?	Yes, you are. / No, you aren't.
Is he/she/it going to play?	Yes, he/she/it is. / No, he/she/it isn't.
Are we/you/they going to play?	Yes, we/you/they are. / No, we/you/they aren't.

Write sentences with *be going to*. Use affirmative (✔) or negative (✗) forms.

1 I / visit my grandma ✔ on Monday
I'm going to visit my grandma on Monday.

2 we / have a party ✔ on Saturday
_____

3 he / travel by ✗ plane
_____

4 they / play football ✗ next weekend
_____

Complete the dialogue. Use *be going to* and the verbs in the brackets.

Elena: We ¹ *are going to have* (have) a surprise party for Amy on Sunday.

Tom: I know. Lucas ² _____ (download) some music.

Elena: Good. I ³ _____ (make) a cake …

Tom: … and buy a present …

Elena: No. I ⁴ _____ (not buy) a present. You ⁵ _____ (go) shopping for the present.

Tom: OK. And Amy and her mum ⁶ _____ (make) pizza I hope.

Elena: Just Amy's mum. Amy ⁷ _____ (not do) anything. It's a surprise party! We ⁸ _____ (not say) a word to her!

3 Put the words in the correct order to make questions. Write short answers.

1 Mum going is to the bank go to ? ✔
Is Mum going to go to the bank? Yes, she is.

2 do you are going to homework your ? ✔
_____

3 Dad play going basketball to is ? ✗
_____

4 Grandma a film see and Grandad going are to ? ✗
_____

5 going Tony to watch a match is ? ✗
_____

✹ 4 Answer the questions for you.

1 Are you going to do your homework on Saturday?
_____

2 Is your mum going to go to work tomorrow?
_____

3 Is it going to snow later?
_____

4 What are your parents going to do tonight?
_____

5 What are you going to do in the summer?
_____

Extra Online Practice

Unit 8, Video and Grammar
www.myenglishlab.com

Revision of questions

You are excited → Are you excited?

You are wearing my clothes. →
Are you wearing my clothes?

You were a good student. →
Were you a good student?

You've got a girlfriend. →
Have you got a girlfriend?

You can rap. → Can you rap?

You want tickets. → Do you want tickets?

She sings. → Does she sing?

You went to Paris. → Did you go to Paris?

Where do you buy your clothes?
What did you have for breakfast?

1 Write questions. Use *he*, *she* or *they*.

1 Carla can dance.   *Can she dance?*
2 Rocco is sporty.   _____
3 Rocco and Big Al were late. _____
4 Carla has got a new bike. _____
5 Big Al is listening to music. _____

2 Complete the questions with *Do*, *Does* or *Did*.

1 *Does* Jane live in London?
2 _____ she visit Italy last summer?
3 _____ Jane and George often play tennis?
4 _____ her dad text her every day?
5 _____ her grandparents call her yesterday?
6 _____ you like pizza, Jane?

3 Match answers a–f to the questions in Exercise 2.

a ☐ Yes, she did.
b ☐1 Yes, she does.
c ☐ Yes, they did.
d ☐ Yes, I do.
e ☐ Yes, he does.
f ☐ Yes, they do.

✽ 4 Complete the questions. Write short answers.

Last week.

1 *Was* he happy? *Yes, he was.*
2 _____ he visit London? _____

Today

3 _____ they painting? _____
4 _____ the dog like the song? _____
5 _____ they got a cat? _____

5 Vocabulary Circle the types of music.

6 Match pictures A–F to sentences 1–6.

1 ☐B David plays classical music with his violin.
2 ☐ My brother plays the guitar and he's in a roc band.
3 ☐ Grandad plays jazz music.
4 ☐ Dave is a reggae singer.
5 ☐ My little sister loves rap music!
6 ☐ Kittens is my favourite pop band.

19 Making arrangements

🔊 **19 Making arrangements**

A: Are you busy next *Thursday*?
I've got tickets for *a basketball match*.
Would you like to come?

B: That sounds great. I'd love to come.
What time does it start?
Where shall we meet?

A: Let's meet outside the *Arena* / at *six o'clock*.

1 Match 1–8 to a–h.

1 [d] Are you   **a** like to come?
2 [ ] I've got tickets   **b** does it start?
3 [ ] Would you   **c** great.
4 [ ] That sounds   **d** busy next Tuesday?
5 [ ] I'd   **e** o'clock at my house.
6 [ ] What time   **f** for a football match.
7 [ ] Where shall   **g** love to come.
8 [ ] Let's meet at five   **h** we meet?

2 Complete the dialogue with one word in each gap.

Maria: Hi Alison. Are you ¹ *busy* next Tuesday?

Alison: No. Why?

Maria: I've got four tickets for a dance show.
² _____ _____ and your mum like to come?

Alison: ³ _____ _____ great. ⁴ _____ _____ to come. Let's text my mum and ask. What time does it start?

Maria: At half past seven. It's at the Old Theatre near the underground.

Alison: Great. Mum texted me and said yes. Where ⁵ _____ _____ meet?

Maria: ⁶ _____ _____ outside the underground station at seven o'clock.

Alison: Great. See you then.

3 Number the dialogue in the correct order.

[ ] **Mark:** What time does it start?
     Gary: At three o'clock. It's at the New Park Stadium.

[1] **Gary:** Hi Mark. Are you busy next Saturday?
     Mark: No. Why?

[ ] **Gary:** Where shall we meet?
     Mark: Let's meet outside my house at half past two.
     Gary: Cool. See you then!

[ ] **Gary:** I've got tickets for a football match. Would you like to come?
     Mark: That sounds great. I'd love to come.
     Gary: Great.

4 What tickets has Gary got? Look at Exercise 3 and tick (✔).

[ ] STADIUM: Park Arena
TIME: 2.30 p.m.
DATE: Sunday

[ ] STADIUM: New Park Stadium
TIME: 3 p.m.
DATE: Saturday

5 Complete the dialogue for the other tickets in Exercise 4.

Anna: Hi, Barry. ¹ *Are you busy next Sunday* ?

Barry: No. Why?

Anna: I've got tickets for a basketball match.
² _____ ?

Barry: That sounds great. I'd love to come.

Anna: ³ _____ .

Barry: What time does it start?

Anna: ⁴ _____ . It's at the Park Arena.

Barry: ⁵ _____ ?

Anna: Let's meet outside my house at two o'clock.

Barry: Cool! See you then.

Extra Online Practice

Unit 8, Video and Communication
www.myenglishlab.com

Running for fun!

Do you like running? Yes?
Well, why not try these fun events?

January: Winter Run!

Where is it? Brown Forest

Who can go? Families

What can you do? You can run one or two kilometres. There's hot soup for the runners after the race! Remember to wear a hat!

March: Fun Races!

Where is it? New Park School

Who can go? Children aged 7–12

What can you do? You can run in three races. You can run in an egg and spoon race, a jumping race or a hopping race. There's a crazy basketball game in gloves in the afternoon.

May: Costume Run!

Where is it? Tree Park

Who can go? Children aged 5–14

What can you do? Put on your favourite costume and you can run 50 m, 100m or 200 m. In the afternoon you can have a picnic with your friends.

Have fun, runners!

1 Read the text. Label the events.

1 _____ 2 _____

3 _____

2 Read the text again. Answer the questions. Write *yes* or *no*.

1 Can families run in all the events? ___no___

2 Is there a hot meal for the runners in the Winter Run? _____

3 Can children over 12 run in the Fun Races? _____

4 Are there three races in the Winter Run? _____

5 Are there three races in the Costume Run? _____

6 Is there a picnic at the Tree Park event? _____

3 Read the text again. Circle the correct answer.

1 Which event is in a forest?
  a Winter Run! b Fun Races!
  © Costume Run!

2 Which event is in a park?
  a Winter Run! b Fun Races!
  c Costume Run!

3 Who can run in the Costume Races?
  a families b children aged 7–12
  c children in costumes

4 What can you do in the afternoon at New Park School?
  a play basketball b have some soup
  c have a picnic

5 What do you wear in the basketball game after the Fun Races?
  a a costume b gloves c a hat

6 What food do you need for the Fun Races event?
  a soup b an egg c an apple

4 Answer the questions for you.

1 What is your favourite running event in the text?
  _____

2 Do you like running?
  _____

3 Can you run 50 metres?
  _____

4 Can you run two kilometres?
  _____

5 Do you think running is better in winter or summer?
  _____

1 🔊 **20 Listen and match the names to the birthday events. There is one extra event.**

1 [F] Tina   4 [ ] Kelly
2 [ ] Harry   5 [ ] David
3 [ ] Robert

A   birthday party at home

B   go bowling

C   go to the cinema

D   eat at a restaurant

E   have a barbecue

F   see a dance show

🔊 **20 Listen again. Complete the sentences with the words in the box.**

brother   dad   mum   ~~sister~~   uncle

1 Tina has a ticket for her ___sister___ .
2 Harry is going to go out with his _____ .
3 Robert's _____ is making a cake.
4 Kelly and her _____ love the same activity.
5 David is going to go out with his _____ .

An invitation

Inviting people:	Please come to … / I'd like to invite you to …
Date and time:	On Sunday, 14th July, at 7 p.m.
The place:	At Ice Planet / At 14 Milton Road
Asking for a reply:	Please reply to …
Other information:	Please bring … Your parents can collect you from …

3 Complete the invitation with the words in the box.

At   August   collect   reply   Please   p.m.   ~~Tuesday~~

Please come to…
George's Pancake Day party

On: ¹Tuesday , 3rd ²_____ , at 4:30 ³_____ .
⁴_____ : Fun Times Sport Centre

We're going to go swimming and then eat pancakes.
⁵_____ bring towels for the swimming.
Your parents can ⁶_____ you from
Patty's Pancakes at 9 o'clock.

Please ⁷_____ to george@gmail.com
or call 6789 54321

4 Read George's invitation again. Answer the questions.

1 What day is the party going to happen? ___Tuesday___
2 Where is the party going to happen? _____
3 What are they going to do first? _____
4 What do they need to bring? _____
5 What are they going to eat? _____
6 What time is the party going to finish? _____

5 Now write your invitation. Use the questions in Exercise 4 to help you.

Check yourself!

Vocabulary

1 Look at the pictures. Complete the sentences.

0 We often have a *barbecue* in the summer.

1 We're watching a very good _____ at the theatre.

2 We're having a _____ in the park.

3 I went to a _____ _____ last weekend.

4 This is the best _____ _____ this winter!

5 This is Jimmy's _____ . He's five today!

☐/⑤

2 Complete the gaps.

A   **B**   **C**

JANUARY **11**   FEBRUARY **23**   MARCH **31**

A There's a ⁰_r o c k_ concert on the ¹_ _ _ _ _ _ _ _ of January.

B There's a ²_ _ _ _ _ _ _ _ _ concert on the ³_ _ _ _ _ _ - _ _ _ _ _ of February.

C There's a ⁴_ _ _ concert on the ⁵_ _ _ _ _ _ _ - _ _ _ _ of March.

☐/⑤

Grammar

3 Complete the sentences. Use the correct form of *be going to*.

0 You *'re going to make* (make) a sandwich.

1 He _____ (listen to) some music.

2 She _____ (not come) to my party.

3 They _____ (not go) on holiday this year.

4 _____ (you / watch) a film after school?

5 _____ (we / meet) outside the station?

☐/❚

4 Complete the questions with one word in each ga▮

0 _Is_ it an expensive car?

1 _____ they playing a pop song?

2 _____ he ride a bike?

3 _____ you go to school yesterday?

4 _____ you got a pet?

5 _____ she like sausages?

☐/❚

Communication

5 Complete the dialogue with one word in each ga▮

Lucas: Hi Elena. Are you busy ⁰_next_ Friday?

Elena: No. Why?

Lucas: I've got tickets for an ice dance show. ¹_____ you like to come?

Elena: That ²_____ great. I'd love to com▮ What time ³_____ it start?

Lucas: At 2 o'clock. It's at the ice skating place.

Elena: Great, where ⁴_____ we meet?

Lucas: ⁵_____ meet outside at 1.30.

Elena: Cool. See you then.

☐/❚

Vocabulary ☐/⑩
Grammar ☐/⑩
Communication ☐/⑤
Your total score ▮ / 25

Unit 8, Language Revision
www.myenglishlab.com

Read Trisha's blog about planning.

Word blog: Weekend plans

1 My photos Circle the correct answer.

What are you going to do this weekend? Post some ideas!

1 **Hannah:** I'm going to organise *a fancy dress / birthday* party for my little sister! Does anyone want to help?

2 **Danny:** I'm going to see a *classical / rock* concert. I've got three tickets. Who wants to come?

3 **Joe:** I'm going to have a *picnic / barbecue* and cook lots of meat. Sausages anyone?

4 **Bob:** My brother is going to do a *rap / pop* song on a TV talent competition! Don't miss it at 7 p.m.!

2 Get more Complete the sentences with the words in the box.

come   invitation   musician   prizes

1 There are many great _____ for the winners.
2 I can't come to the party. I haven't got an
_____ .
3 He's a good _____ . He can play the guitar and the piano.
4 Please _____ to my fancy dress party!

3 My blog Complete the text. Use ordinal numbers.

Planning is fun! On the _____ (1st) day of every month I start to plan. My sister doesn't like planning! After the _____ (3rd) or _____ (4th) day of every month she says 'Oh, is it a new month?'

Last month we had a problem. Mum's birthday was on the _____ (15th) and my sister forgot! It's the _____ (2nd) time she forgets!

Lucky for my sister, I remembered. I bought a present for mum on the _____ (13th). 'Thank you, little sister!' she said. My birthday is on the _____ (28th) of this month. Is my sister going to remember?

Get more words

Surprise! Have a great day, Mum!

Find and circle the differences. In your notebook, write four sentences.

A

B

Photo 1. In A, a boy is cooking sausages, but in B …

Reading and Writing

FUN TIME! How did you spend your last holiday? Did you have fun?

I went to Cambridge with my family for a day. First, we got on a red bus and went sightseeing. I took lots of photos with my new camera. Then we bought food from the market and had a picnic next to the river. After that we went on a boat! That was exciting. I didn't buy any souvenirs because we didn't have time.

Magda, 12

My best day out in the holidays was to the Transport Museum. I went there with my parents and little brother. We learnt lots about the history of transport in the UK. It wasn't boring because there was so much to see and do. We got on and off beautiful old trams and my brother was a bus driver for five minutes!

Michael, 13

There's a small farm near my town for animals with no home. My granny sometimes helps there. I went with her one day in the holidays. There were cats, dogs, hamsters and four horses. The farm looks after the animals and looks for a new home for them. I'm going to help there next summer. I can't wait!

Alice, 11

1 Read the texts. Answer the questions.

0 What did Magda do first?
She went sightseeing.

1 Where did Magda have lunch?
_____

2 Why didn't Magda buy any souvenirs?
_____

3 What did Michael learn about?
_____

4 Who was a bus driver for five minutes?
_____

5 What animals did Alice see?
_____

6 What is Alice going to do next summer?
_____

◯/6

2 Look at the picture. Complete the sentences and answer the questions.

10.15

0 What time does the red bus leave? *quarter past te*
00 The pink suitcase is *next to the plan*
1 The girl in the purple jeans is _____
2 The girl's mum is _____
3 The old woman is wearing _____
4 What's the old woman doing? _____
5 How many suitcases are there? _____
6 What's the man in the green jumper doing? _____

◯/(

Matt is on holiday. Read the notes and help him write a postcard.

0 we / have / a lovely time / France
1 yesterday / we / go / sightseeing
2 mum / buy / some souvenirs
3 I / not buy / anything
4 then / we / have / dinner / at a restaurant
5 tomorrow / I / go / swim in the sea!

Hi Granny,

0 *We're having a lovely time in France.*

1 _____

2 _____

3 _____

4 _____

5 _____

See you soon!

Matt

☐/⑤

istening

🔊 **21 Rosie wants to have a party next weekend but everyone is busy. Listen and match people 0–4 to pictures A–F. There is one extra picture.**

0 ☐C best friend Zara   3 ☐ classmate Brian
1 ☐ cousin Don   4 ☐ Julie from Karate Club
2 ☐ neighbour Jasmine

A

B

C

D

E

F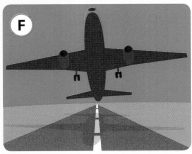

☐/④

Communication

5 Read the sentences and circle the best answer.

0 **Alex:** Are you busy next Saturday?
  Jill: Ⓐ No, I'm not. Why?
       B What time is it?
       C I'd like a ticket, thanks.

1 **Alex:** Would you like to come to a football match?
  Jill: A I can't play football.
       B Yes, I like playing football.
       C That sounds great!

2 **Alex:** Where shall we meet?
  Jill: A At half past two.
       B We can ask John.
       C We can meet outside the stadium.

3 **Alex:** Let's go by bus. It's easy.
  Jill: A Yes, that's a good idea.
       B There isn't a bus on Sundays.
       C I haven't got a bike.

4 **Alex:** How much is the bus ticket?
  Jill: A It's three pounds fifty, please.
       B It's three pounds.
       C At two o'clock.

☐/④

Reading and Writing ☐/⑰
Listening ☐/④
Communication ☐/④
Your total score ▢ / 25

Exam Practice

Look and read. Choose the correct words and write them on the lines. There is one example.

a salad

a swimming pool

a city

a glass

scissors

cheese

a calculator

an island

Example

Many people live here. ___*a city*___

Questions

1 You can drink water from this. _____

2 This can be inside or outside. You can swim in it. _____

3 This food is yellow, orange or white. People often put it on pizzas. _____

4 You can cut paper with these. _____

5 You need this in *Maths* lessons. _____

Part 2 Reading and Writing

Read the text. Choose the right words and write them on the lines.

Animals and food

When people __*are*__ hungry, they eat something. They can eat some fruit
or a sandwich, ¹_____ people often cook the food that they eat.
They like eating chicken and chips or pasta. But what do animals eat? Well,
animals don't ²_____ their food. There are ³_____ animals that
eat meat, for example, lions and tigers. There are other animals that only eat
fruit and plants.
Birds ⁴_____ fruit because it is sweet and everyone knows that
monkeys love bananas. Elephants are much bigger than monkeys and birds
but they ⁵_____ eat meat! They eat fruit and plants too.

Example	is	am	are
1	so	but	because
2	cooks	cooking	cook
3	any	no	some
4	like	likes	liking
5	always	never	often

Part 3 Reading and Writing

Look and read and write.

Examples

The football match is very ___exciting___ .
What is the dog eating? ___sausages___

Questions

Complete the sentences.

1 The woman is wearing a blue _____ .
2 The girl in the grey T-shirt is taking a _____ .

Answer the questions.

3 What is the woman doing? _____
4 Where is the laptop? _____

Now write two sentences about the picture.

5 _____

6 _____

Part 4 Listening and Communication

🔊 22 Listen and draw lines. There is one example.

Ben   Sally   Nick   Kim

Jim   Daisy   Vicky

Part 5 Listening and Communication

Read the text and choose the best answer.

Example

Anna: Hello, Daisy. How are you?

Daisy: (A) I'm fine, thanks.

     B I'm Jill's sister.

     C I'm riding a bike.

Questions

1 Anna: Where are you going?

   Daisy: **A** I'm going now.

       B I'm at home.

       C To the supermarket.

2 Anna: What do you want to buy?

   Daisy: **A** Some eggs.

       B We don't need any flour.

       C I've got some pasta.

3 Anna: I like going to the supermarket.

   Daisy: **A** Yes, please.

       B I'm not sure.

       C I don't.

4 Anna: Do you want to come to my house this afternoon?

   Daisy: **A** No, I like my house.

       B I'd like that, thanks.

       C Where are they?

5 Anna: Let's watch a DVD!

   Daisy: **A** That's a great idea!

       B Yes, I am.

       C Yes, I can.

6 Anna: OK. See you later.

   Daisy: **A** Bye.

       B Yes, I do.

       C That's all right.

Exam Practice

Part 1 Reading and Writing

Read the story. Choose a word from the box. Write the correct word next to numbers 1–6. There is one example.

My name is Fred. I like going to concerts, taking photos and playing _football_ .
At the weekend, I like doing sport. I also like doing things with my family and
friends. Yesterday, my sister and I ¹_____ to the park and played with Dan,
our ²_____ . Some friends from school were at the park. We played games
with them too. Today, my friend John and I ³_____ our bikes down by the
beach. We went for a swim and then came home to ⁴_____ something
because we were hungry. My mum made us some lunch. We had a ⁵_____
and some chips. It was nice but my favourite food is chicken and potatoes.
Tomorrow is Monday so I'm going to do my ⁶_____ now.
Yes, I work and I play at the weekend!

Example

football	burger	walked	eat	homework

dog	rode	jumped	milk

7 Now choose the best name for the story. Tick (✔) one box.

Fred's friends ☐
Fred's weekend ☐
Fred's favourite food ☐

Part 2 Reading and Writing

Look at the pictures and read the story. Write some words to complete the sentences about the story. You can use 1, 2 or 3 words.

A family holiday

Last year, Alex and his sister Sue went to the beach for their summer holiday. They loved it! They went swimming every day and they met other children who they played with. This year they didn't go to the beach. They went to a village in the mountains. It was beautiful but Alex and Sue weren't happy. "We want to go swimming. We want to play games on the beach. I think this place is boring," said Alex.

Examples

Alex and his sister went on a beach holiday last ___year___ .

The children went swimming every day on their ___holiday___ .

Questions

1 This year the children went to _____ in the mountains for their holiday.

2 Alex said the place was _____ .

But on the third day of their holiday, they met a boy called Sam. Sam lived in the
village. He took them to all the exciting places! They went to the cinema with Sam
and to the village park, where they played all day. It was smaller than the park at
home but it was fun. In the second week, they went swimming at the swimming pool.
They started to enjoy their holiday very much.

They met Sam on the _____ day.

The children went swimming and _____ in the village park.

The village park was _____ the park at home.

On the last day of their holiday, Alex and Sue didn't want to go home. They were very
sad. Sam was sad too. He said, "Don't worry. We can chat online. See you next year!"
Alex and Sue smiled. They were happy that Sam was their new friend.

Sam wanted to _____ with the children.

The children were happy because Sam was their _____ .

Part 3 Listening and Communication

🔊 **23** Listen and write. There is one example.

The school trip

Example

Where? _____a farm_____

Questions

1 Teacher's name: Miss _____

2 How many types of animals? _____

3 Favourite animals: the horses and the _____

4 Lunch: _____ and fruit

5 Bought: _____

Part 4 Listening and Communication

Jackie and Meg are school friends. They're talking about birthdays and parties. What are Jackie's questions? Write them on the lines. There is one example.

Example

Jackie: What ___*did you do last Saturday?*___

Meg: I went to Jack's birthday party last Saturday.

Questions

1 Jackie: Was _____ ?

Meg: It was fantastic!

2 Jackie: How _____ ?

Meg: I think twenty people were there.

3 Jackie: Have _____ ?

Meg: Yes, I've got a lot of photos.

4 Jackie: When _____ ?

Meg: My birthday's on May 20th.

5 Jackie: What _____ ?

Meg: I'm going to have a fancy dress party.

Get more on Science!

Taste

1 🔊 24 Listen and repeat. Find the words in the picture.

Vocabulary Taste

bitter   salty   sour   sweet   taste buds
tongue

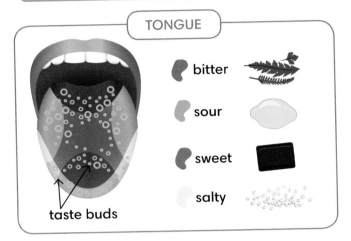

TONGUE

bitter
sour
sweet
salty

taste buds

2 Look at the text. What is it about? Guess. Then read it quickly and check.

The text is about
a the food some people like.
b how people know what food they like.
c how people make their food sweet.

3 Read the text again. Complete sentences 1–4 at the bottom of the page. Use words in Exercise 1.

4 Read the text again. Answer the questions.

1 Where are your taste buds? <u>on your tongue</u>
2 How many different tastes are there? _____
3 What is there in sweet food? _____
4 Are lemons sour or bitter? _____
5 Why do some people put sugar in tea? _____

5 What do these food items taste like? Put the words in the box in the right places.

chips   dark chocolate   ~~jam~~   lemons
milkshake   sausages   strawberries   yoghurt

sweet: <u>jam</u> , _____ , _____
salty: _____ , _____
sour: _____ , _____
bitter: _____

6 What is your favourite taste? What food has this taste?

My favourite taste is _____ .
_____ *have / has* this taste.

SWEET OR SALTY?

How do you know that biscuits are sweet and chips are salty? Because you've got lots and lots of taste buds. Where are they? Right there – on your tongue.

When you put food in your mouth, it goes on your tongue. The taste buds on your tongue tell you what taste each type of food has.

There are four different tastes: sweet, salty, sour and bitter. Food with sugar is sweet. When you eat milk chocolate or cakes, the taste buds in the front part of your tongue tell you that they are sweet. Salty food has salt on or in it, like cheese on pizza. What is a sour taste? Well, drink some lemon juice! That's sour! And the taste buds in the back part of your tongue tell you what's bitter. Black tea is bitter. Some people put sugar in their tea because they don't like the bitter taste.

1 Lemons are <u>sour</u> .

2 Chocolate cake is _____ .

3 Black tea is sometimes _____ .

4 Pizza is _____ .

🔊 **25 Listen and repeat.**

Vocabulary National parks

canyon ☐ cave ☐ geyser ☑ 1 glacier ☐
hot spring ☐ peak ☐

Read the text quickly. Match photos 1–6 to the words in Exercise 1.

American National Parks

Yellowstone National Park is the first national park in the world. You can do a lot of exciting things there. You can sail on the rivers and swim in the lakes. But be careful about some hot springs. They are colourful lakes with hot water. In some hot springs the water is too hot to swim. Sometimes this hot water goes high up in the air and you can watch exciting geysers. Lots of people take selfies next to them. You can also take photos of beautiful waterfalls – you only need to walk in the canyon.

Many people visit the **Glacier National Park** to see one of its 25 glaciers. A glacier is moving ice. The park is also popular because of its mountains. The peaks – the tops of the mountains – are high. Climbing is dangerous so it's better to look and take photos or try to find some caves in the mountains! There are lakes and rivers so you can sail a boat. You can ride horses with your family and in winter you can go skiing.

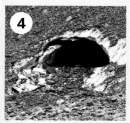  

3 Tick (✔) the geographical features you read about in the text.

	Yellowstone National Park	Glacier National Park
canyon	✔	
cave		
geyser		
glacier		
hot spring		
lake		
peak		
river		
waterfall		

4 Read the text again. Complete the sentences with the words in Exercise 1.

1 At Yellowstone National Park people like taking selfies next to the exciting _geysers_ .
2 You can walk in the _____ to see some waterfalls.
3 The water in a _____ can be very hot.
4 At Glacier National Park there are 25 _____ .
5 The _____ of the mountains at Glacier National Park are high.
6 You can go into a _____ in a mountain.

5 Which is your favourite national park: Yellowstone or Glacier? What can you see there? What can you do there?

My favourite national park is

_____ .

You can see _____ .

You can _____

in this park.

Get more on Art!

Different forms of art

1 🔊 26 Listen and repeat.

> **Vocabulary** Different forms of art
>
> exhibition   graffiti   jewellery   painting
> photography   sculpture

2 Complete the plan of an art museum with the words in Exercise 1.

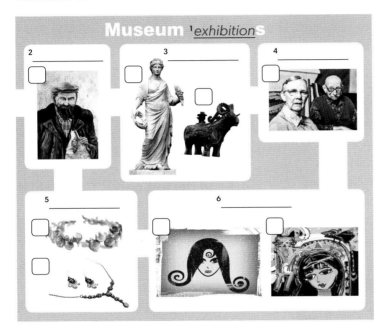

Museum ¹_exhibition_s

2
3
4
5
6

3 Read the text. Which works of art did Beth and Mark like best? Tick (✔) the photos in Exercise 2.

> ✕   Art blog   ≡
>
> **The Metropolitan Museum of Art is in New York. It is the biggest museum in the USA. Beth and Mark visited the museum last Saturday.**
>
> **Beth**   I liked the sculptures best because I think art from the past is very interesting. There was a beautiful sculpture of a woman that I really liked. There was also an exhibition of glass jewellery. I don't like wearing anything on my fingers or in my ears but that jewellery was amazing. The jewellery from yellow glass was my favourite.
>
> **Mark**   I want to be an artist so I loved the paintings. There were some paintings of people with animals that I liked a lot. I also liked the photography exhibition and I thought the black and white photos were the most interesting. But my favourite exhibition was about graffiti. Some people say graffiti is bad writing on walls, but I don't agree. The best one was of a girl with long purple hair. That was awesome!

4 Read the text again. Complete the sentences with one word in each gap.

1 The Metropolitan Museum of Art is the _biggest_ museum in the USA.

2 Beth really liked a beautiful sculpture of a _____ .

3 Beth also liked the glass _____ .

4 Mark wants to be an _____ .

5 Mark's favourite exhibition was about _____ .

5 Which words do you connect with these forms of art? Complete the table. Use the words in the box and add your own.

> animals   beautiful   cheap   difficult
> easy   expensive   glass   metal
> new   old   paint   people   wall

painting	
photography	
graffiti	
jewellery	
sculpture	

6 What is your favourite form of art? Where can you see it?

My favourite _____ .

I can see it _____ .

Flying machines

1 🔊 **27** Listen and repeat.

> **Vocabulary Flying machines**
>
> biplane   engine   glider   hot-air balloon
> kite   wing

2 Read the text. Find and underline the words in Exercise 1.

A short history of flying

The first flying machines were kites. The Chinese made them about 1500 years ago. They were usually triangle-shaped.

Then, there was the hot-air balloon. A fire under the balloon made the air hot. In November 1783 two men flew a hot-air balloon in France for about 8 km.

But people wanted to fly like a bird so they made gliders – flying machines with very big wings. In the 1890s they flew about 100 or 150 metres.

People wanted to fly a longer way so in 1902 in America the Wright brothers made a biplane. It had two long wings. One wing was at the top and one was under it. And a year later, they made a biplane with an engine – the Wright Flyer. Biplanes with engines flew a long way but people needed bigger planes.

This happened in the 1950s. The British, Russians and Americans made planes for many people. They had big engines in or under the wings and they flew a very long way.

3 What flying machines are they? Label the photos with words in Exercise 1.

1 _____

2 _____

3 _____

4 _____

4 Read the text. Match the dates to the flying machines.

1 ⟨ f ⟩ 1500 years ago   **a** biplane with an engine
2 ⟨   ⟩ 1783   **b** glider
3 ⟨   ⟩ 1890s   **c** big plane with big engines
4 ⟨   ⟩ 1902   **d** hot-air balloon
5 ⟨   ⟩ 1903   **e** biplane with no engine
6 ⟨   ⟩ 1950s   **f** kite

5 Read the text again. Circle T (true) or F (false).

1 They made the first kites in China.   Ⓣ/ F
2 In 1783 there were three people in the
  hot-air balloon.   T / F
3 We made the first flying machine with
  wings before the first hot-air balloon.   T / F
4 The Wright brothers made a flying machine
  with an engine.   T / F
5 Biplanes had long wings.   T / F
6 In the 1950s only the Americans
  made big planes for many people.   T / F

6 Answer the questions.

1 Do you like flying kites?

_____

2 Do you think flying in planes is fun?

_____

3 Do you want to fly in a hot-air balloon?

_____

4 What is your favourite flying machine in the text?

_____

Answer key

Get started! Check yourself!

Exercise 1

1 sofa 2 hoodie 3 bath 4 T-shirt 5 fridge

Exercise 2

1 November 2 Turkey 3 funny 4 February 5 skateboard

Exercise 3

1 hasn't 2 isn't 3 are 4 can 5 can't

Exercise 4

1 Her 2 their 3 are 4 isn't 5 that

Exercise 5

1 from 2 Spanish 3 England 4 is 5 October

1.7 Check yourself!

Exercise 1

1 d 2 e 3 f 4 c 5 b

Exercise 2:

1 play 2 gym 3 canteen 4 do 5 hall

Exercise 3

1 play 2 watches 3 doesn't have 4 don't go 5 don't do

Exercise 4

1 I always do ballet on Monday.

2 He sometimes walks to school.

3 I never play football before school.

4 Do you have a sandwich for lunch?

5 How often is she late in the morning?

Exercise 5

1 What's your name?

2 How do you spell it?

3 Where do you live?

4 What's your phone number?

5 What's your email address?

2.7 Check yourself!

Exercise 1

1 tomatoes 2 jam 3 bread 4 flour 5 potato

Exercise 2

1 jar 2 bottle 3 bar 4 packet 5 can

Exercise 3

1 some 2 a 3 any 4 – 5 an

Exercise 4

1 How much 2 How many 3 How many 4 How much
5 How much

Exercise 5

1 I'd 2 Would 3 Anything 4 Can 5 thanks

Skills Revision 1&2

Exercise 1

1 A 2 C 3 C 4 B 5 A 6 A

Exercise 2

1 usually 2 tuna 3 dinner 4 don't 5 make 6 food

Exercise 3

1 (His favourite subject is) Science.

2 (It's on) Tuesday and Thursday.

3 (His favourite sport is) karate.

4 (Karate is his favourite sport) because it's cool.

5 (Karate Club is) in the gym.

Exercise 4

1 C 2 C 3 B 4 A

Exercise 5

1 Where do you live?

2 What's your email address?

3 Would you like a drink/anything to drink?

4 Would you like some chips?

3.7 Check yourself!

Exercise 1

1 camera 2 TV 3 am good at 4 scared of 5 tablet

Exercise 2

1 text 2 take 3 surf 4 online 5 download

Exercise 3

1 is sending 2 isn't/is not doing 3 are wearing 4 aren't
having/are not having 5 am running

Exercise 4

1 Is she making 2 Yes, I am. 3 Is Tom sitting
4 No, we aren't. 5 Are your parents watching

Exercise 5

1 here 2 speak 3 afraid 4 Just 5 See

4.7 Check yourself!

Exercise 1

1 forest 2 volcano 3 desert 4 mountain 5 lake

Exercise 2

1 friendly 2 difficult 3 fast 4 expensive 5 safe

Exercise 3

1 easier than 2 more difficult than 3 better than
4 more expensive than 5 hotter than

Exercise 4

1 This pizza is the cheapest meal.

2 This is the best holiday of all.

3 This is the worst ice cream.

4 My sister is the most beautiful person in my family.

5 You are the most intelligent student in my class.

Exercise 5

1 favourite 2 about 3 think 4 In 5 right

Skills Revision 3&4

Exercise 1

1 good at 2 (new) puppy 3 worried about 4 microchip
5 see 6 big

Exercise 2

1 river

2 the red boat/one

3 biggest

4 (She is) taking a selfie.

5 (She's wearing a white) T-shirt and shorts.

6 (The woman/ She's wearing) (an orange) dress and a hat.

Exercise 3

1 The shark/It is surfing.

2 The girl / She is running.

3 Shark City is the most expensive.

4 No, it isn't. It's easier (than Volcano Disaster).

5 Desert Adventure (is the newest game).

Exercise 4

1 waterfalls 2 highest 3 seventeen/17 4 dangerous

Exercise 5

1 A 2 B 3 A 4 C

5.7 Check yourself!

Exercise 1

1 police station 2 boring 3 between 4 stadium
5 busy

Exercise 2

1 library 2 café 3 sports centre 4 train station 5 theme park

Exercise 3

1 were 2 was 3 was 4 weren't 5 wasn't

Exercise 4

1 Was 2 were 3 wasn't 4 we were 5 they weren't

Exercise 5

1 Excuse 2 straight 3 Turn 4 Go 5 on

6.7 Check yourself!

Exercise 1

1 doctor 2 farmer 3 chef 4 a shop assistant 5 bus driver

Exercise 2

1 empty, bin
2 walk, dog
3 wash, car
4 look after
5 do, shopping

Exercise 3

1 studied 2 cycled 3 stopped 4 played 5 cleaned

Exercise 4

1 met 2 drank 3 bought 4 took 5 gave

Exercise 5

1 sorry 2 if 3 fine 4 please 5 all right

Skills Revision 5&6

Exercise 1

1 F (last weekend) 2 T 3 F (he took them)
4 T 5 F (on Saturday) 6 T

Exercise 2

1 post office 2 surprised 3 waiter 4 bag 5 ran

Exercise 3

A boring café

Exercise 4

1 My photos were fantastic!
2 Mum made a yummy pizza for lunch.
3 Dad gave me my pocket money.
4 We went to the cinema in the afternoon.
5 We watched the film and ate ice cream.

Exercise 5

1 E 2 D 3 A 4 F

Exercise 6

1 d 2 a 3 e 4 c

7.7 Check yourself!

Exercise 1

1 backpack 2 taxi 3 hotel 4 sightseeing
5 sleeping bag

Exercise 2

1 by car 2 takes, photos 3 by bike 4 eat, restaurant
5 off, bus

Exercise 3

1 didn't go 2 didn't take 3 didn't wear 4 didn't study
5 didn't stop

Exercise 4

1 Did he leave
2 Did your dad cook
3 Yes, she did.
4 Yes, he did.
5 No, they didn't.

Exercise 5

1 please 2 Here 3 How 4 does 5 arrive

8.7 Check yourself!

Exercise 1

1 play 2 picnic 3 sleepover 4 football match
5 birthday party

Exercise 2

1 eleventh 2 classical 3 twenty-third 4 pop 5 thirty-first

Exercise 3

1 He's going to listen to
2 She isn't going to come
3 They aren't going to go
4 Are you going to watch
5 Are we going to meet

Exercise 4

1 Are 2 Can 3 Did 4 Have 5 Does

Exercise 5

1 Would 2 sounds 3 does 4 shall 5 Let's

Skills Revision 7&8

Exercise 1

1 Next to the river.
2 She/They didn't have time.
3 The history of transport in London.
4 Michael's (little) brother.
5 Cats, dogs, hamsters and four horses.
6 Help at the farm (for animals).

Exercise 2

1 reading (a guidebook)
2 eating a sandwich
3 a hat and a (pink) dress
4 taking a photo
5 two
6 getting off a/the blue bus.

Exercise 3

1 Yesterday we went sightseeing.
2 Mum bought some souvenirs.
3 I didn't buy anything.
4 Then we had dinner at a restaurant.
5 Tomorrow I'm going to swim in the sea!

Exercise 4

1 E 2 A 3 F 4 D

Exercise 5

1 C 2 C 3 A 4 B

Irregular verbs

Infinitive	Past Simple	Infinitive	Past Simple
babysit	babysat	leave	left
be	was, were	lose	lost
blow	blew	make	made
break	broke	meet	met
bring	brought	put	put
build	built	read	read
buy	bought	ride	rode
come	came	run	ran
cut	cut	say	said
do	did	see	saw
draw	drew	send	sent
dream	dreamt, dreamed	sing	sang
drink	drank	sit	sat
drive	drove	sleep	slept
eat	ate	speak	spoke
fall	fell	spell	spelt, spelled
feel	felt	spend	spent
find	found	stand	stood
fly	flew	swim	swam
forget	forgot	take	took
get	got	tell	told
give	gave	think	thought
go	went	throw	threw
grow	grew	understand	understood
have	had	wake up	woke up
hear	heard	wear	wore
know	knew	win	won
learn	learnt	write	wrote